The English
LAKE
DISTRICT

Molly Lefebure

HASTINGS HOUSE, PUBLISHERS,
NEW YORK, 22

First published in the United States of America 1964

© Molly Lefebure, 1964

MADE AND PRINTED IN GREAT BRITAIN BY
WILLIAM CLOWES AND SONS LTD, LONDON AND BECCLES

TO MY FATHER

*who taught me my way round the Lake District
and how to read a map*

CONTENTS

THE ILLUSTRATIONS

The Illustrations

ACKNOWLEDGMENT

The Author and Publishers wish to thank the following for permission to reproduce the illustrations appearing in this book:

J. Allan Cash, for figs. 7–9, 14 and 16.

Leonard and Marjorie Gayton, for figs. 3, 19, 24 and 25.

Noel Habgood, for figs. 1 and 2.

A. F. Kersting, for figs. 5 and 13.

G. Douglas Milner, for figs. 15, 21 and 22.

Ministry of Public Building and Works, for fig. 6 (Crown Copyright).

The Mustograph Agency, for figs. 10, 11, 18, 30 and 31.

W. A. Poucher, for fig. 32.

Sanderson and Dixon, for fig. 33.

Jack Scheerboom (Joan Wickes), for fig. 4.

Kenneth Scowen, for figs. 12, 17, 23 and 26–9.

Sylvia Treadgold, for fig. 20.

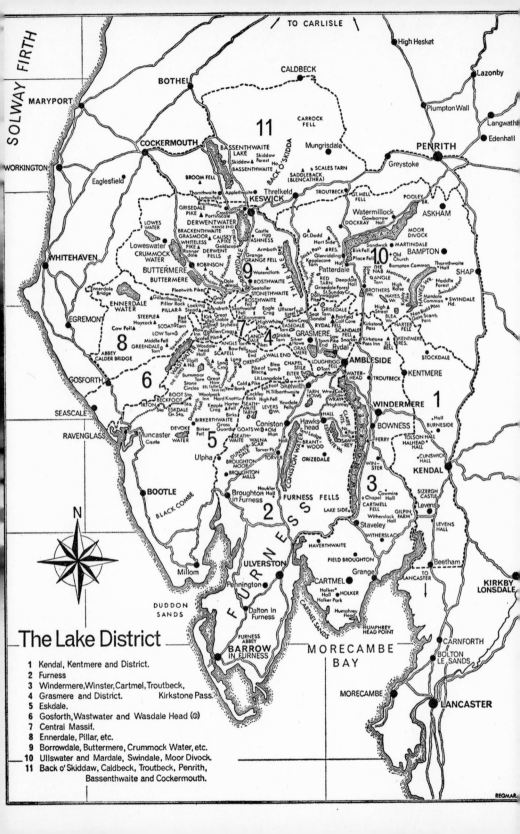

The Lake District

1 Kendal, Kentmere and District.
2 Furness
3 Windermere, Winster, Cartmel, Troutbeck,
4 Grasmere and District.   Kirkstone Pass.
5 Eskdale.
6 Gosforth, Wastwater and Wasdale Head (0)
7 Central Massif.
8 Ennerdale, Pillar, etc.
9 Borrowdale, Buttermere, Crummock Water, etc.
10 Ullswater and Mardale, Swindale, Moor Divock.
11 Back o' Skiddaw, Caldbeck, Troutbeck, Penrith,
    Bassenthwaite and Cockermouth.

CHAPTER ONE

A Way In

'One hurried journey, though it be through the midst of it, is apt to establish a very false impression. The true one is only gained by lingering and leaving the beaten tracks.'   J. M. Baddeley (B.A.)

'The journey of he who walks is a hundred times better than the journey of he who rides.'   Mahommed

'Perhaps there is some justification for each generation to have a new book describing the Lake District and revealing themselves.'   Frank Singleton

'. . . time cannot erase; . . . presence and absence, definitive as they may seem, are part of a larger process . . . the effects of our actions are endless.'   John Berger

You will search in vain for lakes. Meres and waters and tarns abound, but strictly speaking there is not a genuine lake from Ennerdale to Mardale, from Bassenthwaite to Coniston. The word 'lake' does not exist in the indigenous tongue of the district; nobody spoke of lakes until the first tourists came, headed by Thomas Gray, poet and traveller, jolting and swaying in a coach from whose windows he was several times too frightened to look, a charming man who had his leg pulled by the natives, as indeed all strangers have their legs pulled, however politely, even today. Gray returned south to talk of lakes, and the habit spread; thus you get people speaking of Lake Derwentwater or of Buttermere Lake and so on, which is quite unnecessary and indeed wrong; but there it is, these northern waters are dubbed lakes, and the land they are found in has become famous as the Lake District. It is too late to change things now.

The lakes are in actual fact but secondary features in this district; it is the fells which play the leading role. To those who live here or spend any real time here the fells are living individuals of whom one speaks in friendly, albeit respectful, terms: 'Skiddaw has snow on him still . . . Great Gable is looking wonderful this morning . . . The Old Man is angry tonight.'

Worn by the elements and time the Lakeland fells sprawl like giants who have become drowsy over the ages. However, if disturbed, they raise heavy heads and rumble, like lazy but annoyed old lions, while in spite of their age they occasionally spring and claim a victim; usually some foolish tourist who has failed to treat them with the proper respect. However inanimate they may appear to the dull or unobservant they are without doubt alive; if this sounds ridiculously fanciful let me say it is a fancy common to all who know these fells intimately. A most up-to-date doctor to whom I recently lamented that man now has the power to blow these formerly eternal hills to bits replied with conviction: 'Oh, Great Gable would never allow that to happen, you know. He would come striding down to the House of Commons and put a stop to all that.'

The vital statistics of these hills are insignificant when measured against those of other ranges, but people who have climbed from the Alps to Nepal will tell you that the sensation of being upon and amongst mountains can be experienced in the Lake District as strongly as anywhere. This is because the Lake District is a great mountainous region reduced to miniature, the reduction in size carried out so perfectly to scale that every peak, pass and valley is in exactly related proportion, thereby achieving a brilliant *trompe d'œil* effect. Travelled visitors who come expecting mere mole-hills are confounded.

Much of the magic of the district also lies in a wonderful kaleidoscopic quality that can make the landscape change in appearance not only from day to day but virtually from hour to hour. Dorothy Wordsworth's *Journal* provides the best-known written evidence of this. Each day she took the same walk, each day she described a different scene. On one spring Thursday she found it, 'A very fine morning. The sun shone . . . Rydale was full of life and motion . . . the lake was covered all over with bright silver waves.' Next day it was rainy; she gathered mosses. On Saturday when she awoke 'the whole vale was covered

2 *Ashness Bridge and Derwentwater, with Skiddaw in background*

with snow'. Sunday was showery, Tuesday was a mild morning, Wednesday she and William walked to Rydale and 'it was a beautiful spring morning—warm, and quiet with mists'.

There is a letter from Coleridge, written from Keswick, in which he says that he has often thought of making a set of playbills for the district, for every day of the year, announcing the performances by his Supreme Majesty's servants, 'clouds, waters, Sun, Moon, Stars, etc.'.

Therefore, reader, do not despair if you fail to have heat-wave weather while in the Lake District; you will see more beauty and more changes in landscape than you would under an endlessly blue sky. For, to quote Coleridge again, '. . . in settled fine weather there are none of those goings on in heaven which at other times give these scenes such an endless variety. . . . Summer is not the season for this country . . . then it is like a theatre at noon.'

In other words you should, if possible, avoid visiting the district during what is known as the bracken-season. This extends from the end of June until the end of September; during these months the fellsides, at other times so varied in form and colouring, are engulfed in a monotony of green fern, their contours and features blurred thereby, if not wholly obliterated. This quite apart from the complaint that, if the weather is hot, the district is like a theatre at noon, with the alternative, of course, that if it does rain the downpours of July and August are of such a particularly solid, persistent nature that the district then resembles Regent's Park Open Air Theatre trying to put on *A Midsummer Night's Dream* in a deluge.

The bracken remains unfurled until the end of June while by the end of September it has withered to blazing gold and bronze. The best months of all for the Lakes are April, May, early June and October.

As for the best way into the district, opinions vary. The late intrepid H. H. Symonds, who, though I never met him personally, was and indeed still is my great friend by dint of nearly 30 years of treading the fells with his book for company,[1] made no bones about how his readers should enter the district. Taking up his pen he commenced briskly and bluntly: 'Some enter the district by motor, which does the district a disservice; you yourself will doubtless come by train.'

Not only did he expect his readers to come by train; he expected

[1] H. H. Symonds, M.A., *Walking in the Lake District* (Chambers).

3   *Borrowdale from Brund Fell*

them to get out at Penrith, or Shap, from there to walk with him west-wards across the whole district for several days.

Alas, times have sadly changed. You, my reader, will doubtless come by motor-car, your intention to tour the district in that same vehicle. Of course, to be brutally frank, you cannot possibly hope to see the Lake District properly by car; even today walking is still the only real way in which to see this part of the world. Indeed there are many places in the district that cannot be reached except upon foot. How-ever, I will not belabour the point. Here and there I shall suggest you should get out of your car and walk; I can do no more than that.

If you come northwards by road you are almost bound to come into the district by Kendal, which is the way that Mr Baddeley commends. It is at this point that I think I should introduce you properly not only to Mr Symonds but to the other two people who make up a celebrated and indispensable trio of Lakeland guides. All three were eminent, Victorian in the best sense of the term, outspoken, decided in their views and a trifle tetchy, as highly distinguished and respected old gentlemen usually are. Symonds wrote his book in 1933; he was the best walker of the trio and a fine writer; the early editions, especially, of his book are treasured not only as guides but as good reading.

M. J. B. Baddeley, B.A., was the author and compiler of the most detailed and famous guide ever written to the Lakes;[1] Symonds refers to him repeatedly. Mr Baddeley lived at Windermere in the last half of the last century; there is a memorial clock-tower to him at the road-junction half way between Windermere Station and Bowness Pier; in my mind's eye, let me confess, I envisage M. J. B. Baddeley as a man looking very much like this actual clock-tower. As a guide Baddeley does indeed possess the virtues of a good clock; he never misinforms you, never fails to instruct you correctly and promptly whenever you consult him.

In real life he was indefatigable as a walker and traveller, sincerely loving the beauties of Lakeland. His personality is best summed up by the story of his bustling and tireless organisation of the district's celebrative beacons at the time of Queen Victoria's Diamond Jubilee; he climbed Scafell Pike four times in the course of the great day to tend the fire up there. Finally, when he died, several years later one

[1] Baddeley, *Guide to the Lake District* (Ward, Lock & Co., Ltd).

hastens to add and not as a result of his Jubilee exertions, stones were 'conveyed with great labour from the summit of Scafell Pike' for his grave in Bowness cemetery.

A well-used Baddeley guide-book is generally curved into an odd boomerang-shape through being carried year in year out crammed into the sodden pocket of an anorak or rucksack. The remaining maps are tattered and fastened with little bits of adhesive paper, the cover is blotchy and slightly mildewy, while compression and damp have welded the pages into a solid *papier-mâché* composition so that the book will no longer open at any but a few special places; each owner's book, as it solidifies, decides for itself at which few pages it will consent to open. In the end it won't open anywhere, is no longer anything more than a solid paper brick which you carry with you for tradition's sake; the time has then come to take your old Baddeley and give him decent burial on Maiden Moor or High Raise, after which you buy yourself the latest edition which at first you handle reluctantly, thinking of dear dirty soggy old edition-whatever-it-was lying up there on the fell, under a sod of sphagnum-moss.

Early editions of Baddeley are treasured (when in good enough condition to be readable) for their information about where to hire a pony-and-trap at fourpence an hour or where to lodge for the night at one-and-sixpence, breakfast included.

Finally there is Professor W. G. Collingwood, author of *The Lake Counties*, a very large and heavy book you could not possibly carry about with you in your pocket. The Professor was a great personal friend of Ruskin in the days when Ruskin was living, sick and ageing, at Coniston. Collingwood's book deals with history and folk-lore rather than with the fells, his style is romantic and he quotes a great deal of Wordsworth rather indiscriminately, but his pages contain a mass of fascinating and erudite information which makes wonderful base-camp reading.

So with Symonds who walks, Baddeley who talks and Collingwood who digs up the past you really cannot go wrong.

Baddeley says that if you travel northward by road you should enter the district by Kendal, although both he and Collingwood criticise this entry-route on the grounds that everyone takes it and it has become a 'sheep through the gap' way in. Hogg-hole though it may be (you shall learn presently what a hogg-hole is) entry by Kendal *is* very convenient;

it also introduces you first to the lowlands of the Lake District, through parts where men were living and working long before they penetrated the mountain dales to live and work.

You may like to visit Lancaster before you proceed to Kendal, Lancaster being an historic and attractive old town with a hill-top castle dating back to William I. It was once a place of importance. From it you will pass into a countryside associated, peaceful and pastoral as it now looks, with Border warfare and Scottish raids.

The Lake District lies within three counties; Lancashire, Westmorland and Cumberland. It is a small, miraculous area of hill country which was conceived under a shallow coral sea 500 million years ago, raised by earthquakes, shaped by ice and the elements and finally populated by Vikings and a particular breed of sheep, the Herdwick, whose precise origin is unknown.

I fear you must face a little geology as you now drive towards these distant, hazy-blue hills amongst which you will soon be staring and, I should like to think, sweating. It is pleasant to visualise you bounding out of your car to climb the mountains because they are there, but you should also have at least a basic notion of how they got there in the first place.

It is, of course, a complicated tale. The Lake District took a long long time to become the wonder that it is; detailed preparation and slow, loving cooking form the essentials of many a great dish, as anyone who has prepared a *Bisque d'Ecrevisses* or *Bœuf en Daube* will tell you. Gastronomically speaking I should perhaps cite a tatie-pot as more appropriate in this particular context; surely there is no dish more delicious, when slowly and tenderly and lusciously cooked, than a classical Cumbrian tatie-pot?

First, then, in the preparation of the Lake District came the Skiddaw Slate, which started as the sludgy mud-rock bed of a warm shallow ocean 500 million years ago. Fossilised, this mud-rock now forms most of the District's northern mountains with Black Combe, fell of folklore and fairies, as an unexpected outcrop in the south of Lakeland. Bassenthwaite, Crummock and Loweswater are all enfolded by Skiddaw Slate, Derwentwater and Buttermere almost entirely so, Ennerdale and Ullswater partly so too. Skiddaw and Saddleback, Grisedale Pike, the Newlands Fells, Grasmoor and the Whinlatter Fells are all of this fossilised fabric; they are among the oldest mountains in the world.

After the mud-rock of the shallow silting sea came volcanoes, discharging vast showers of lava, ashes and debris, which now form the fabric of the so-called Borrowdale Volcanic Rock of the central *massif* of Scafell and the Pikes, Gable, Honister, the Langdales, Helvellyn and High Street, Borrowdale, Upper Eskdale, Wasdale, Dunnerdale, Upper Patterdale and Mardale. But, let me repeat, do not think you are looking at actual extinct volcanoes when at last you find yourself in Borrowdale or at Wasdale Head, or perhaps standing on Scafell's great Pike, the highest point in England (all of 3,162 feet); you are looking at incredibly ancient volcanic debris that has been carved and sculptured by natural forces over millions of years.

This volcanic debris formed a hard crust over the original mud-rock which now bent into folds and tented up into a dome. After which mighty effort the dome then subsided under a warm sea again and the embryonic Lake District returned, so to speak, to Square One.

Next formed what is now the Coniston Limestone, composed of volcanic waste and a mixture of pebbles and coral from the shallow, all-embracing sea. There is not a great deal of this Coniston Limestone; it mainly runs in a thin belt from the Duddon Estuary across the district to Shap.

The sea deepened, then silted up again; thus the Silurian slates and grits were formed. These are found almost entirely in Westmorland, providing the scenery round Windermere and the greater part of Coniston; a tender, pretty, happy landscape. This Silurian group is the youngest of the four major rock groups of the Lake District; 360 million years old, or thereabouts.

Earthquakes now tented these four rock groups into a great pyramid. Molten rock masses boiled and seethed, forming those odd pockets of granite, granophyte, gabbro and the rest which appear unexpectedly in various parts of the district (one learns these things in detail best by rock-climbing, for then it is a matter of genuine interest, say, that granite dries quickly after rain, that gabbro skins your finger-tips as you climb).

Now the future Lake District lay hoisted up in the air and for 50 or 60 million years the elements gnawed at it and peeled it, as Herdwick sheep in a hard winter gnaw bark from trees. Then everything sank under water again.

This new sea in its turn silted up, steamy tropical forests of giant ferns and feathery-foliaged trees grew, crashed with old age into the mud from which they had sprung, fossilising to form the Whitehaven-Maryport coalfields. The ever-rising ground dried out, becoming bare and hard; a desiccated land which we now greet as Old Red Sandstone. Fresh earth upheavals raised the Old Red Sandstone and the rest into a new and enormous dome. Once again the elements with tireless hands and teeth massaged and gnawed the dome's surface away; back to light came the Silurian rocks, the Coniston Limestone, the Volcanic rocks and the Skiddaw Slate, now with an irregular band of Carboniferous rock around the edges. Debris from the centre of the dome dispersed on to the outer rim to form New Red Sandstone.

The dome, wearing over the ages, sank lower. This was a landscape of naked, fantastic, sun-baked, gully-scoured mountains below which stretched plains with sand-dunes and shallow lagoons. Here lived creatures called labrinthodonts; their footprints have been found in Penrith sandstone.

The land sank, the lagoons spread, soon everything was under water again. But this new ocean silted up in due course, exactly as the earlier oceans had done. Sand vanquished everything; now the future Lake District was a desert. This in its turn succumbed to water which turned the desert into a steamy swampland; for the next 100 million years everything was very wet and warm and monster reptiles bred, animated mountains of flesh crawling and swimming and inheriting the mud.

Then, a mere 50 million years ago, there were fresh and horrible earth convulsions and up from the swampy sea the land rose again, in appearance slightly more like the Lake District we know today; a huge tilted rock-wheel with an outward drainage movement of valleys and spurs.

The elements commenced their work again of rubbing, gnawing and scouring until, perhaps a million years ago, the climate became so cold that the snow no longer melted in summer and vast snow-fields and glaciers covered the land. The valleys filled with ice which grew thicker and rose higher and higher until there was a great sea of ice with solitary peaks protruding from it. The First Ice Age was established.

Palaeolithic Man, huntsman and cave-artist, was now flourishing in warmer climates, but understandably he rarely ventured North, except during those intermittent periods between recurrent Ice Ages when the snow-caps thawed a little.

All the while the grinding, remorseless glaciers, in their endless advances and retreats, were carving out the U-shaped Lakeland valleys and the little so-called 'hanging' valleys; these latter you will see today as small high valleys from which you descend generally by a steepish drop, with maybe a waterfall, to a lower, broader U-valley below, or as curved corries at the dale heads, or on the flanks of the mountains. From these hanging valleys flowed the glaciers in sluggish motion.

The lakes themselves, narrow and deep, were either formed in basins carved out of the rock by ice, or enclosed by dams of moraine.

The last Ice Age probably came to an end about 20,000 years ago. Since then the elements have continued to chisel and smooth the shapes of the fells. Even as we look at them today changes are imperceptibly going on; the wind, the rain, in winter the frost, ice and snow, in summer the heat of the sun, all work ceaselessly on the fell faces. Fragments of crag chipped off to collect in screes, crags cracked as they expanded after frost, water gradually washed every surface smoother and flatter. The weather fingers the fells incessantly, like a blind man ceaselessly reading Braille, but we ourselves, transient creatures, never live long enough to grasp the full significance of the natural changes going on, so that, like Coleridge, we say, 'Blessings to the mountains! To the eye and ear they are always faithful.'

Faithful, that is, unless we build over them, run mountain-railways up them, park caravans and cars at their feet and generally behave like Yahoos.

The first men to live here were the Stone Age people; they made their homes in the lower country, journeying into the fells to quarry stone for their axes and implements. Large numbers of discarded axe-heads have been found in the screes below Pavey Ark, above Stickle Tarn, particularly. Stone Age settlements have been discovered on the edge of the district; the best known is near Beckermet on the Cumberland coast.

Celtic Man of the Bronze Ages followed. The Bronze Age people were megalith builders; they came most probably from the coasts of

France and Spain and they built stone circles and menhirs. The best-known stone circles are at Castlerigg, near Keswick, Long Meg and her Daughters near Penrith and the Swinside stone circle on the lower slopes of Black Combe; all three very well worth visiting. However, there are many other lesser known circles and remains; these one tends to discover on lonely ambling days, days when one pursues no exact set course, but prowls happily over some lonely stretch of fell, going where the going takes you. One circle, found in such a manner, is a small isolated ring, with traces of a ditch and embankment, standing on the windswept side of Burnbank Fell; I recall it with pleasure.

There are Bronze Age burial places on Burnmoor above Eskdale, on Moor Divock above Ullswater and a settlement and numerous burial cairns at Barnscar near Devoke Water, with fortified positions on higher ground nearby. To all these we will presently go, if you are willing to walk.

The once celebrated Shap Stones or 'Karl Lofts' seem to have been a magnificent megalithic monument of two stone circles and a mile-long avenue of menhirs; reminiscent, almost, of Carnac. Unfortunately there was a time, not so long distant, when the local people regarded such collections of stones as stocks of free building material and so, of the famous Shap Stones, only a few isolated ones now remain.

Cumberland and Westmorland were occupied by the Brigantes, a warlike tribe who probably continued to live here under Bronze Age conditions long after the rest of England had entered the Iron Age and was under the Romans.

Signs of their settlements can be seen at Kentmere, at Heathwaite near Coniston and Lanthwaite Green near Crummock Water. Hill-forts have been found at Castle Crag overlooking Haweswater, at Peel Wyke on Bassenthwaite and there is a queried fort, or fortified settlement, in Rannerdale not far from Lanthwaite Green, while others have been found in the neighbourhood of Derwentwater.

The Romans, when they arrived, formed an alliance with the Brigantes and it was not until the Brigantes themselves broke the alliance that the Romans had to impose order upon the tribe. After the Romans left came a period of native territories and kingdoms. Then came Christian missionaries, anxious to convert these heathen. Some two or

three centuries later came the Norsemen; they liked the look of this
country, it reminded them of home. They colonised it and settled; it
is thought more than probable that it was they who introduced the
Herdwick sheep. The descendants of these men and their sheep still
dwell in the dales today.

And you, reader, are by this time on the doorstep of Kendal,
secretly vowing that you won't be caught traipsing over Burnmoor and
Black Combe with me looking for burial-cairns and stone circles,
neither do you intend coming with me on one of my lonely ambling
days. Well, that may be; I never argue with my prospective victims, I
simply appear armed with a packet of Kendal Mint and pass the observation that it is time to start. Moreover, as my sister remarks, I have so
far brought all my victims back alive. It is true that we have memories
of one or two corpse-like creatures staggering into the yard feebly
calling for water. . . . However, you are nowhere near that part of the
journey yet, you are driving into Kendal, a most attractive and highly
civilised town.

Kendal and Kentmere

Kendal, Kentdale. Most people hurry through convinced that they have not yet arrived in the Lake District; they will not consider themselves arrived until they glimpse Windermere. Guide-books confirm them in this attitude with the warning that although Kendal is 'the gateway to the Lakes' the visitor must not expect, at Kendal, to find himself in the Promised Land. 'Kendal is several miles distant from the Lake District proper.'

Is it? This depends entirely upon what one means by 'the Lake District'. There are many people (more, probably, than one cares to suppose) who, hearing the magic words, have flash upon their inward eye that view of Friar's Crag, Derwentwater, which graces the lids of so many toffee-tins and fudge-boxes. There are others who walk the fells year in year out until they have their topography by heart, could tread the Drumhouse route to Green Gable blindfold, know Fairfield or Helvellyn better than the back of their hand, as they will proudly tell you, but even they have not discovered the Lake District which is something much more than a beautiful land for walkers, something more than a National Park. Men dwell there, as well as mountains, the district has a great history besides great views, there is very active indigenous life going on beneath the veneer of tourism and Lovely Lakeland. This is a part of the world which has always produced, still does produce, people who are intensely individualistic, often out-standing. A surprisingly large number of distinguished men have been born in this district, from John Dalton to Joe Bowman. The place has an immensely varied past. You know nothing of Lakeland if you have not heard of the Redmans, the Radcliffes, the Bellinghams, the Gilpins, the Lawsons or the Barwicks. You must know something of mines, be able to discourse upon the use of the stope and feather, be able to differentiate between a hogg, a shearling and a twinter, gimmers and wethers, know what to expect on a clarty day.

You, my reader, virgin to the whole field and now pacing rather impatiently beside the River Kent, can take it that you have at last in truth reached the Lake District, even if there is as yet no lake to stare at. There is plenty here in this land of Kentdale which is far more relevant to the District than nine-tenths of what you will meet with at Bowness or Grasmere.

Shortly before you reach Kendal, some five miles south of the town, you will notice on your left a garden crowded with ancient and fabulous topiary-work overlooked by a large old house. This is Levens Hall. The house, the oldest part of which dates back to 1188, is open to visitors on Thursday afternoons, the gardens are open daily. Walking between the centuries-clipped pagodas and peacocks you will find yourself sinking into a ruminative mood; this is altogether a ruminative part of the world.

Until the seventeenth century this Border country was always under the threat of northern invasion and always difficult to defend because of the easily navigable Morecambe Bay with its three estuaries of the rivers Kent, Lune and Leven. The ancient British had numerous camps overlooking the Kent valley, the Romans built fortresses against invaders from the sea, while later the local people erected farmsteads protected by pele-towers; square, thick-walled towers with a vaulted provision-room on the ground-floor, a narrow-windowed room above for look-out and defence and a living-room over that. Warning of approaching invaders was given by a system of beacon fires. When the marauders drew close the villagers seized their valuables, deserted their wattle-built cabins, drove their cattle into hiding places, then crowded into the pele-tower for safety.

Yew-trees were planted in all the churchyards, not to provide the melancholy shade so much approved of in later centuries by romantics, but to furnish bows for the archers. All able-bodied males between the ages of sixteen and sixty were obliged under the terms by which they held their land, 'Border tenure', to give their aid, whenever required, in repelling the invaders. Sometimes reprisals took place, then the invaded became invaders.

The Redmans bought the Manor of Levens from Ketel, Baron of Kendal, in 1188 and built the pele-tower together with a great hall, kitchens and so forth; a Plantagenet dwelling of substance. Matthew de Redman, in 1305, was summoned, together with one John d'Ewyas, both as elected knights of the county, to serve in Parliament (the first regular English Parliament was convened in 1295). To the statement of their election both knights affixed their marks, neither of them being able to write. It took six days, in either direction, for them to make the journey between London and Lancaster, eight in snow or foul weather. Expenses might be claimed for the journey.

Once established politically the Redman family carried on the tradition of service to their country, both in civilian and military spheres. Sir Matthew Redman, who died in 1360, sat for Westmorland in the parliaments of 1357 and 1358. His son, also Sir Matthew, served in France and Spain under John of Gaunt, while the grandson, Sir Richard Redman, became Speaker in the House of Commons.

The Redmans sold Levens to Alan Bellingham of Burneside in 1489 and moved to their manor of Harewood (today the home of the Earl of Harewood). In 1585 Sir James Bellingham followed the fashionable course of wealthy Tudor men and set about converting his old Plantagenet house into a fine modern mansion; fortunately part of the old pele-tower, however, can still be seen.

A central tower was built at the front of the house, the ancient Great Hall and kitchens were replaced by an impressive entrance hall with fine oak and plaster work, a Spanish-leather covered dining-room named 'The Guilt Parlour', two drawing-rooms and the famous Bellingham staircase, which led to a series of handsome bedrooms. In 1689 another Alan Bellingham sold the house to Colonel Grahme, M.P., Privy Purse to James II and later Deputy-Lieutenant for Westmorland. Desirous of making Levens the envy of the North, Colonel Grahme had the gardens laid out by the designer Beaumont, who had been working on the grounds of Hampton Court for James II. The Levens gardens today remain almost exactly as Beaumont designed them.

But Colonel Grahme left no male heir to this home he was so proud of and it passed into the Bagot family. For over two centuries there was no direct male heir to Levens; the result, it was said, of a curse which a beggar, refused alms and refreshment, had placed on the house, pronouncing that no male heir would be born until the river Kent ran dry and a white stag appeared in the Park. In 1896 the river Kent froze solid and an off-white stag was born in the Park; in February 1896 a Bagot heir was born. Levens still remains in the Bagot family.

Irrelevant literary associations are the bugbear of the Lake District. Many authors of whom the modern tourist has never heard, let alone read, come trooping from all directions to prattle about what they have written; the perennial failing of all authors. Therefore, if I give her half the chance, from Levens Hall will come lumbering Mrs Humphrey Ward, a lady of intimidating *embonpoint*, grand-daughter of the fearsome Dr Arnold of Rugby. She aches to tell you that while staying at Levens Hall she wrote *Helbeck of Bannisdale*, using this locality as a setting for her novel; if you do not watch out she will start reeling off the titles of all her other books, but you will have to cut her short for you will never see anything of the real Lake District if you take up all your time with spurious literary associations. Helbeck is a phoney, his like never trod these local dales or any other. So let us leave Mrs Humphrey Ward; she will be furious to find herself thus dismissed, but it can't be helped. Of course, if you happen to have read her books and you enjoyed them you will want to linger, talking to her, but forgive us if we leave you; we shall be at Sizergh Castle.

Sizergh Castle, the home of the Strickland family, boasts a fourteenth-century pele-tower. Katherine Parr, sixth and last wife of Henry VIII, was a great friend of the Stricklands and often visited here; a specimen of her beautiful needlework has been preserved, making her presence seem especially real and touchingly near to us. Like all proper castles Sizergh is haunted. It is also famous for its sixteenth-century panelling, although the best of this has now been removed to the Victoria and Albert Museum in London. The castle is open to the public on Thursday afternoons in summer; you could possibly visit both here and Levens on the same afternoon, though this might not give you much time to linger over the delights of either place.

Other noted pele-towers in the locality are Nether Levens, Dallam Tower, the remains of Beetham Hall, a fourteenth-century fortified house, and Arnside. Beetham church is one of the oldest in the district and contains rather battered effigies of the last Thomas de Betham, Knight of the Shire for Westmorland in 1425, and his lady.

So into Kendal. Here too the houses were built with an eye to defence, being grouped round yards gained by a gateway from the street, a gateway that could be securely bolted and barred. Most of the houses have been rebuilt, but still around the old yards. There are several seventeenth-century houses surviving in Kendal, a few date from even earlier, while there is much eighteenth-century building.

The Romans, whose steps we shall be able to trace across the district, had a fort here, situated on their road from Lancaster to Ambleside, their Galava.

'Kentdale' was granted by William Rufus to his baron, Ivo de Taillebois, in recognition of services rendered. The Taillebois family survived, slowly declining throughout the centuries, until 1861 when the last of the line, Emily Taillebois, an eighteen-year-old pauper girl, died in a Shrewsbury workhouse; a Dickensian death-bed scene indeed.

The old town was guarded by the castle, now in ruins but worth visiting none the less. At this castle Katherine Parr was born. One can imagine this rather plump and charming young woman travelling from Kendal Castle to Sizergh to visit her Strickland friends, taking her needlework with her, and prayer-book too. The needlework you have already seen at Sizergh, the prayer-book is now kept at Kendal Town Hall.

Most of the north of England turned gaily out to defeat the Scots at Flodden Field in 1513. In the old ballad the King appoints the Earl of Surrey as Regent of the North and tells him about the various forces he can expect to have united under him to fight the Scots, including,

> . . . *the Bower of Kendall bold,*
> *Which ferce will fight, and never flee.*

But not only Kendal responded to the call for men:

> *And all that clim the Mountayne came,*
> *Where groune from Frost is seldom free,*
> *With lustie ladds, and large of length,*
> *Which dwelt on Sommer water syde.*

The Border warfare came to an end with the accession to the throne of James I of England, VI of Scotland, son of Mary Queen of Scots. James spent the night in Kendal on his journey south. A hundred and forty-two years later, during the '45 Rebellion, Prince Charles

Edward Stuart slept in Kendal on his way south with his invading Highland army, and slept there again six weeks later in the course of his
retreat. The next night he moved on over Shap summit to sleep at a
farm; his guns with his rearguard under Lord George Murray were
now in Kendal. The Duke of Cumberland's army, outnumbering the
Jacobites by six to one, was in lumbering pursuit. By next night
Charles had reached Penrith, the guns were on Shap, and Cumberland
was in Kendal, occupying the same house, the same bed even as that
graced by the fleeing Prince two nights previously. We are told that
the Prince had complained that he was overcharged for his night's
board and lodging; the Duke appears to have left no comment.

Next day the Highland guns reached Penrith, and late that evening
a rearguard skirmish took place, in the dark, on the edge of Clifton
Moor outside Penrith, in which the Highlanders got the worst of things
and were obliged to withdraw. They had laid their ambuscade round
Town End, the house of one Thomas Savage, a Quaker (this house can
still be seen). During the fighting the Quaker and his daughter firmly
shut themselves up in their house, but when the trouble was over they
emerged to provide 'Butcher Cumberland' (as he was soon to be
known in Carlisle and throughout the Highlands) with dinner and a
bed, Savage 'rejoicing much in the Spirit that such a Guest was come
under his Roof'. He found the Duke 'pleasant, agreeable company',
which was more than most people did.

Prince Charles Edward and his officers were meantime spending the
night at Penrith in a house that is now part of the George Hotel.

Clifton church Register contains entries recording the burial of
those killed in the skirmish, including one Highlander who, buried
several days later, doubtless died of wounds.

Cumberland's main difficulty was that he could not bring up the
English troops quickly enough to intercept Charles because there were
no roads worthy of the name in the locality. After the Highland
invasion the Whig government started building roads in the north;
'Wade's Road', built by General Wade from coast to coast on the line
of the old Roman wall, is commemorated in the jingle:

> *If you'd seen this road before it was made*
> *You'd thank the Lord and General Wade.*

Hauling their guns with astonishing tenacity and skill the Highlanders were able to reach Carlisle without being stopped by the Duke, and from thence they went over the Border.

Carlisle had surrendered to the Prince upon his entry into England and he had been proclaimed James III in the Market Place; the keys of the city had been presented to him by the mayor and corporation. For this Carlisle now paid dearly. The Duke of Cumberland occupied the city, but the garrison at the Castle held out against him. He bombarded it; when at last the garrison surrendered the Duke treated the rebels with terrible ferocity; the leading officers were hanged, drawn and quartered while their men, together with hundreds of other followers of the Stuart cause, were imprisoned in the Castle dungeons, then hanged in batches. Cumberland is not remembered joyfully in Cumberland.

Kendal's church of Holy Trinity dates back in foundation to the thirteenth century. In 1189, during a particularly savage Scots raid, the townspeople fled into the church for refuge; the invaders followed them into the building and massacred them there. This was not the only scene of violence the church was to see, though the second was of a different nature, not without its lighter side. There are chapels of the Strickland, Bellingham and Parr families in the church, added in the late fifteenth or early sixteenth centuries. Near the Bellingham chapel hang a sword and helmet, said to have belonged to 'Robin the Devil', a lively member of the Philipson family. The Philipsons formerly owned and lived upon Windermere's Belle Island. During the Parliamentary War (always referred to in this part of the world as the Troubles, or the Time of the Troubles) the Philipson brothers took up arms for the King. The elder became a colonel, the younger was a jaunty major; his spirited behaviour won him his 'Robin the Devil' title. One Colonel Briggs, a Kendal magistrate who had joined Cromwell's army, besieged Major Philipson on Belle Island for eight months, at the end of which time Colonel Philipson came to his brother's assistance and raised the siege. The following Sunday the daring Major, accompanied by a small force of mounted supporters, rode into Kendal and, understanding Briggs to be in church, posted his men round the building while he himself, armed, rode down the nave looking for his enemy. One can imagine the effect that this dramatic entry of clattering horse and sword-brandishing rider must have had upon the congregation. Colonel Briggs was not in church after all; an attempt was made to arrest the Major who, trying to exit by riding from a smaller door at the further end of the church, had his helmet knocked from his head by the low archway. Presumably he also dropped his sword; at all events helmet and sword still hang in the church.

But Kendal, in spite of the turbulence of the times it has lived through, is essentially a town of steady industry and thriving day-to-day normality. Its civic history is particularly well-known because of the famous *Kendal Boke of Record*, dated 1577. A flourishing market town from the first, Kendal became renowned for its wool and cloth industries. Milk-white cloth was a Kendal manufacture in much demand during the fifteenth and sixteenth centuries; even more so was the celebrated 'Kendal green': apparently a pleasing shade of bottle-green. Students of Shakespeare will remember Falstaff's 'three misbegotten knaves in Kendal green' who came at him when 'it was so dark, Hal, that thou couldst not see thy hand' and Prince Henry's rejoinder, 'Why, how couldst thou know these men in Kendal green, when it was so dark thou couldst not see thy hand?'

The woollen industry first began to decline in the reign of Elizabeth I; the celebrated Kendal cloths started to go out of fashion in London, then gradually elsewhere. A further blow fell on the industry when the Plague came to Kendal and the district; many of the wool-workers died, particularly the cottage-weavers in the Langdales. Some recovery was made, but the trade was next threatened by machinery. Hand-weaving and knitting had been important additional sources of income to the poor of the countryside, but by 1817 hand-loom weavers were unable to compete with machine weavers. The industry moved from dale cottages to Kendal factories and some of these still do well, but the industry is now nothing in comparison with what it was 300 years ago and more.

But if the wool and cloth industry has declined, Kendal's other traditional industries have not. Kendal has been famous since the seventeenth century for the manufacture of snuff, particularly a type known as 'Kendal brown'. This snuff trade is still going strong, with special triumph for 'Kendal brown'. The old Kendal boot and shoe industry also flourishes.

Kendal has a renowned library and an excellent Museum; this latter you should visit if you can possibly manage the time; the wool and cloth section is particularly interesting. The old grammar school, founded in 1588, has numbered some famous names amongst its pupils. The painter, George Romney, lived in Kendal; he seems to have started his career as a commercial designer for his first known work is a sign for Kendal post-office, a hand posting a letter. Gough, the blind botanist, contemporary of Wordsworth, was another distinguished Kendal personality. De Quincey worked in Kendal as editor of the *Westmorland Gazette* from 1818 to 1820; we shall meet with him again in these pages. Wordsworth, Southey, Professor Wilson, John Dalton, Professor Sedgwick and Dr Birkbeck are among the famous men who have been members of the Kendal Literary and Scientific Society, formed in those civilised days when the arts and the sciences had not yet severed social connections.

In the eighteenth century as many as 350 pack-horses would pass through Kendal in a week. In 1786 the first mail-coach ran to London, in 1846 the railway opened. The modern age had arrived for Kendal.

Before we move out of Kendal, into the Kentmere country which lies beyond, I must not forget to introduce you to Kendal Mint Cake, that delicious sweetmeat no true mountaineer ever travels without and which Hillary and Tensing nibbled on the summit of Everest.

So now, tasting your first Kendal Mint Cake, you move on, exploring. Other famous old houses in the Kendal neighbourhood include Tolson Hall, built in 1630 by Thomas Tolson, a Kendal tobacco merchant and Burneside Hall (the name derived from the Norse 'Brunolf's Head'), a fourteenth-century defensive dwelling with a late sixteenth-century gatehouse; it was formerly the seat of the Burneshead family. During the reign of Edward II the Bellinghams lived there before moving to Levens Hall and greater circumstance. Burneside then passed into the hands of the Braithwaite family of Ambleside. Thomas Braithwaite became Recorder of Kendal; his son, Richard Braithwaite the poet, born in 1588, was and indeed in academic circles still is famous for his bi-lingual poems, written in both English and Latin. The most famous poem, *Drunken Barnabee's Itinerary*, has gone into nearly 20 editions, the most recent appearing in 1932. The Braithwaites, like the Philipsons, were staunch Royalists. They sold

36

4 *Castlerigg Circle, near Keswick*

their house after the Civil War (or, as we must remember to say, the Troubles) and today it is a farm.

Near the road to Long Sleddale is fourteenth-century Selside Hall, once the home of Thomasine Bellingham, Lady Thornburgh, who kept an account-book, dated 1579, which shows the 'holle year waigs' for all her servants at a total sum of £14 10s.; pay for servants numbering 17.

Fifteenth-century Skelsmergh Hall and the rebuilt Cunswick Hall were the homes of the Leyburne family, which ended with John Leyburne who had his estates taken from him as forfeit for taking part in the Jacobite '15 Rebellion.

The vale of Kentmere until a century ago had a small mere, which was ultimately drained. In 1955 and 1959 oak dug-out boats were found here; thought to date back to 1300 or so and built for four or more oarsmen. There is one of these boats on view at the Greenwich Maritime Museum.

Kentmere Hall was the home of the famous Gilpin family. The estates were given to soldier Richard Gilpin by King John. Richard Gilpin, besides achieving fame on the battlefield, was acclaimed hero in Kentmere for killing a savage wild boar which terrorised the valley, after which a boar's head became a feature of the family crest.

Gilpins include George, a minister of Elizabeth I and Bernard his brother, Rector of Houghton, celebrated for his generosity and Christian good works. He refused the bishopric of Carlisle because he felt he could do more useful work in his own parish. He died in 1583 having held the living at Houghton for some 30 years. There are many tales about his piety and acts of charity.

After the Troubles Kentmere was lost to the Royalist Gilpins, but the family continued to produce distinguished sons; among them Sawrey Gilpin, an outstanding equestrian painter who in 1773 was elected President of the Royal Society of Artists. He was brother of the Reverend William Gilpin, an educational reformer who ran a progressive school at Cheam, much in advance of its time and was author of one of the earliest guide-books on the Lakes, *A Tour in the Mountains and Lakes of Cumberland and Westmorland*. Of this guide we shall perhaps hear a little more later.

Sawrey's son, William, painter and landscape gardener, in 1804

39

became first president of the Old Watercolour Society. John Bernard, son of the Reverend William, settled in Massachusetts, where he established a line of notable U.S. Gilpins.

It is said, but I do not know upon what grounds, that John Gilpin, that citizen of credit and renown who made one of the world's most famous rides, was also a member of the Kentmere Gilpin family. I should like to think so.

Kentmere Hall has become a farm-house, its fourteenth-century pele-tower has long since fallen into disuse, old sycamore-trees guard the homestead now, not from Border-marauding Scots but from the wind and rain.

There is some of the most rewarding walking in the district at hand here; fascinating and lonely. The walk up Kentmere will take you to the Nan Bield Pass and Mardale (*Bield* is Norse for shelter and is not the surname of a girl called Nan). The dalehead under Ill Bell is dark and impressive (Ill is pronounced Eel; it is, with Eel, a derivative of E'il, evil. You will come across Ill Crags, Eel Crags, Eel tarn; you are not dealing with eels but with places dark and foreboding). High Street lies beyond, a wonder land for walkers.

Then there is Long Sleddale, peaceful and narrow, enclosed by Goat Scar and Buckbarrow and leading to Harter Fell and Gatesgarth Pass with Haweswater the other side of it.

From Kentmere you can also walk the Carburn Pass to Troutbeck or climb up to Small Water and Blea Water, two delightful and relatively little-known tarns. In the other direction lie the Shap fells; windy and very lonely indeed. This is a part of the district which reveals the true essence of Lakeland as well as any, indeed better now than most, for it is a part which is largely untouched by tourists. Most of it has to be explored on foot, too; a great advantage. If you are a walker, the genuine article, and have not tried the Kentmere district and the fells of Shap then make time, some time, to do so. From the Kentmere and Shap fells you can easily gain the great High Street range; this is the best and happiest territory for the walker now, for these fells remain roadless and lakeless and therefore, by the majority, unheeded. Here, still, are lonely, even desolate places, not only out of season but in season too. I am saying no more, but search on foot and ye shall find.

This sojourn in and around Kendal has, I hope, left you with a good taste in your mouth, making you eager for more. Dramatic historical events, fascinating local industries, some notable houses and families, a large number of interesting people and lastly some beautiful and unspoilt country for walking over; you would have missed all this if you had gone dashing on to Windermere.

Before you go there is one more local character you should meet, a Crossthwaite (Kendal) farmer named Jamie Muckelt. Westmorland and Cumberland are famous for their native humour; the wit is dry, the philosophy embodied in it is pithy and the style of delivery is poker-faced. There have been several noted wits who have also been rhymesters. Muckelt was particularly noted in the vale of Kent for his humorous verses which bubbled from him spontaneously and effectively; whatever the occasion Muckelt was equal to it. There is no room here, unfortunately, to quote him at length; I like, and hope you will like, this specimen, a notice he posted up beside his pea-patch:

> *Pray ye, nebbers, dunnet pul;*
> *I'll gi' ye a pey-scode when they're full.*
> *If ye it 'em when they're swash*
> *They'll fill yer belly full o' trash.*

CHAPTER THREE

Furness

Furness lies in Lancashire; that area of Lancashire north of Morecambe Bay which encroaches upon and finally becomes part of the Lake District.

After the Norman invasion of England in 1066 several large religious houses were founded on English soil by Norman barons; houses which were virtually overseas colonies of the great religious houses of France. In 1123 the Benedictine monastery of Savigny established a colony at Tulketh, near Preston in Lancashire and in 1127 this colony took over, in remote Icelandic-speaking Furness, a grant of properties which had been made by Stephen of Blois (later King Stephen) for the setting up of a monastery. A party of monks left Tulketh to settle in a lonely, almost hidden valley named, in Icelandic, Bekangesgill, or the Vale of Deadly Nightshade. The intrepid pioneering monks erected a tiny settlement of wattle-huts beside the stream which flowed through Bekangesgill and started to build a church. From this simple start flowered the magnificence of Furness Abbey.

The country needed the monks. The lowlands were harassed by Border warfare, while within the high dales lay a wild, dark country which Christian missionaries had penetrated here and there to found small chapels; the dalesmen, descendants of the Norsemen who had arrived some time in the early tenth century, had now reached that stage where their own mythology had become inextricably mixed with the Christian gospels; a confusion beautifully demonstrated by the great Viking cross (*circa* 1000) in Gosforth churchyard, which on one side depicts the Norse demon-god Loki struggling with the serpent while on the other side is Christ crucified.

By 1148 the monks of the new abbey of Furness had built the presbytery of their church, side chapels and some of the adjoining monastery
buildings, according to the architectural traditions of the Benedictines.
The monastery, shortly after this date, was transferred to the Cistercian
Order and the buildings already erected had to be partly demolished
and rebuilt on Cistercian lines; for instance the frater (refectory) with
its Benedictine axis of east to west had to be pulled down and made part
of an enlarged cloister, while a much larger frater was built on the
Cistercian axis of north to south. Gradually the rest of Cistercian
Furness grew up around the nucleus buildings; dedicated, like all
Cistercian houses, to the Virgin Mary.

The lands and possessions of the Abbots of Furness were enormous,
indeed Furness was rivalled only by Yorkshire's Fountains Abbey. To
Furness were affiliated religious houses and monastic institutions as far
distant as Corcomroe, near Galway; closer to home were the daughter-
abbeys at Calder in Cumberland and Shap in Westmorland. The possessions of Furness included fisheries in Morecambe Bay, at Windermere and Coniston, mills, mines, farms, sheep-granges, deer-parks,
forests, quarries, bloomeries, a saline-spring at Manesty in Borrowdale, a flourishing wool-trade, a shipping-trade. The Abbot of Furness
was a personage of enormous power; in all matters civil, ecclesiastical
and military he was supreme, subject only to the King insomuch as he
was bound to furnish the Crown with arms and men when a general
levy was ordered. The Furness legion consisted of four divisions: 'one
of bowmen horsed and harnessed; bylmen horsed and harnessed;
bowmen without horse and harness; bylmen without horse and harness.'[1]
This force was raised by the Abbot from amongst his tenants.

Apart from this obligation to furnish the Crown with arms and men
when called upon to do so the Abbot had all manner of rights, according to Stephen's charter: 'with sac and soc, tol and team, infangene-
theof, and everything within Furness, except the lands of Michael le
Fleming.' The Abbot's lands and tenants were exempt from all
'talliage, toll, passage, pontage, and vectigal'.[1] The Abbot of Furness
was even granted a coroner of his own, chiefly to hold inquests into the
deaths of travellers drowned crossing the notoriously dangerous sands
of Morecambe Bay.

[1] *Antiquities of Furness.*

To facilitate transport throughout the District the monks opened up an artery of pack-pony routes over the passes. These tracks were in much better condition in the pack-pony days than they are now. Careful examination of the Sty, for instance, the famous pass between Borrowdale and Wasdale, reveals remains of a cobbled causeway in the upper, level stretch between Taylor Ghyll Force and Sty Head Tarn, while the terracing of the old, left-hand route down to Wasdale Head is still discernible. Indeed most of the major passes were probably roughly cobbled in their more level stretches; without doubt monkish road-gangs, so to speak, spent the summer months keeping the tracks over the passes in good repair.

These mediæval routes were, after the Dissolution of the monasteries, maintained in good condition by the mining companies and the wool-traders; it was only when the pack-horse trains ceased in the early nineteenth century that the passes became neglected as we know them today.

Over bogs and mosses so-called floating-roads were used; long corduroys, as they are named, of birch-twigs or heather bound into faggots and laid two or three deep in the pathway. Some of these floating-roads were already ancient when the monks came: laid down by the Brigantes, then surfaced by the Romans when they arrived to use them. Such floating-roads were constructed and used until late into the last century.

The major tracks over the open fells, too, were first marked by the monks, either with thorn-bushes or white stakes, planted at regular intervals, or by stone-cairns. Summit cairns (a summit cairn is locally known as 'a man') are, generally speaking, of much later date, though one or two are quite old. The great spate of cairns arrived, of course, with the modern fell-walkers.

Besides making pack-pony ways the monks constructed pack-pony bridges, still a great feature of the district. The earliest of these date back to the late fifteenth or early sixteenth centuries; monk-built, they are narrow and have slightly pointed arches, although when erected they had no parapets. The later bridges built in the seventeenth and eighteenth centuries had low parapets; of these low parapets you will today discover some lingering examples, but most of the bridges you see have had parapets added, or their originally low parapets heightened.

Many of the stone walls you see clambering over the fells were built by the monks. Some are boundary walls, marking heafs (each flock of sheep has its own heaf, or share of fell), some are built to prevent sheep from straying over dangerous crag. In the dale-bottoms are the stone-walls of the intake-fields, dating back to the earliest settlers. The building of these intake-walls achieved a double purpose, that of clearing the ground and marking out the fields. There is no doubt that some of the walls in the Lake District are a thousand years old or more.

Thus the dales were explored and the passes between them opened up by the monks; farming and mining were developed by them, the wastes were charted and tracked, chapels, halls, hospitals, schools and courts came into being; in short it would not be an exaggeration to say that the monks civilised the District.

When you visit Furness Abbey today, some five miles or so inland from Barrow, you will not be obliged to ring the bell of the great gate-house, for the heavy metal-studded oak doors long since vanished, although you can see the marks of their hinge-sockets in the massive stone gateposts. No monks advance to ask you your business. If you are a woman you will not be prevented from entering these once wholly masculine (or, as we shall see, almost wholly masculine) precincts; you will not be directed to the little *capella extra portas*, built in the thirteenth century for females, strangers and other persons not admitted into the monastery. You will pay your entrance money at the custodian's hut and thereafter be free to walk about the abbey ruins, even into the Abbot's lodging.

It was a very wet morning one early May when I arrived there, approaching from the Dalton direction, trudging through the rain peasant-wise, thereby experiencing all the excitement of a mediæval traveller, when, on rounding a bend in the narrow, almost concealed valley into which I was descending, I suddenly saw the abbey, anticipated it is true, but completely overwhelming in its size and red-sandstone beauty.

The cup-like hollow in which the abbey stands has a railway and a road running through it—there is also a modern inn—but despite these intrusions the ruins themselves possess a peace, an atmosphere of pensive tranquillity which seems miraculously inviolable.

'I never thought anyone would come today', said the custodian as I presented myself, dripping water, at the door of his little hut. I paid my admission, and bought an itinerary and description of the ruins. The custodian offered to lend me a pair of wellington boots; I tried them on, they were too large. The custodian suggested trying to wear the wellingtons over my own shoes; I experimented and got a shod foot wedged in the wellington. This was a foolish start to what I hoped was to be a great aesthetic experience. Finally, the wellington boots utterly rejected and the custodian all mackintosh-clad, we issued together from the hut and made a tour of the ruins. The rain fell steadily, with a soft yet strong sound; among the fresh-foliaged trees and bushes of the abbey grounds birds called. The itinerary and description was soon pulpy between my fingers, too wet to be unfolded or read. I returned to the custodian's hut and paid another sixpence for a dry itinerary.

The custodian, a Furness man it transpired from conversation, had played among and upon the ruins as a small boy. 'It was a wonderful playground, you could climb all over the buildings then; that was before it came under protection as an ancient monument.' In those early days he had had no curiosity about the history of his sandstone playground; not until many years later, retired from the Royal Navy and returned to Furness as one of the custodians, had he developed interest in and enthusiasm for the abbey. Now, he confessed, he had a passion for the place.

We talked, the rain abated, blackbirds flew down from the hawthorns and paraded on the lawns. I returned to the ruins which the custodian, who had scrambled about them monkey-wise in childhood, now guarded devotedly from wilful scratch or scrape.

A great wall enclosed, still encloses, the abbey demesne; within these walls were home-pasture, kitchen gardens, orchards, apiary, rick-yards, granaries, woodstores and all other appurtenances of flourishing husbandry. Mills were erected downstream, together with a pack-pony bridge; this bridge is still in existence over the stream and is of a very early type, narrow and without parapets.

The buildings themselves comprised the wonderful church, chapter-house, cloisters, fraters, dormitories and quarters for lay-brothers and novices as well as for the monks, book-closets, monks' parlour, warming-room, latrines, infirmaries, offices, kitchens, butteries,

Abbot's lodging, cemetery, stables, guest-houses, school, great gate-house and the exterior chapel. The abbey was a world sufficient to itself; the way of life there was unquestioned; the monks could not have doubted that Furness was rock-secure. Those monks who were at the abbey in the early sixteenth century looked back down centuries of orderly security and prosperity for Furness, without doubt they looked with complete confidence into the future; they themselves would die, would be buried, would be forgotten, but the centuries would hold security and strength for all future monks of Furness, indeed for all monks. That a King of England would break away from Rome, that the monasteries would close, that they, the monks, would walk the highway as beggars were a thought beyond the bounds of rational speculation. Yet, Dissolution came. Ten thousand secluded celibates were sent to seek their fortunes in the wide world, with only a handful of shillings and a new gown between themselves and complete destitution. The world in its cruelty swallowed them up as if they had never been holy men.

The threatened suppression of the monasteries, looming in the north in 1535, aroused an insurrection, called the Pilgrimage of Grace and led by one Robert Askew, who in his proclamation to the people of Hawkshead styled himself the Earl of Poverty. This rising was dispersed. Three abbots, sundry priors and monks who had played active parts in the movement were executed and further steps were taken to make the suppression of the monasteries total. Roger Pyle, the Abbot of Furness, together with his monks, was charged with raising up a rebellion against the King's Majesty, with giving false information to the Commissioners, and with protecting one of the monks, a Henry Salley who had said that no secular knave should be head of the Church and of another who had gone so far as to say that Henry VIII (the secular knave) was not even rightful heir to the throne.

The Abbot and these monks were taken into custody. Abbot Pyle demanded full investigation of the charges preferred against him and his monks and this was carried out, with the final result that the investigator, the Earl of Sussex, had to report to the King that 'nothing treasonable or indictable could be brought against the house of Furness'. However a way still had to be found whereby 'the said monks might be ryd from the said Abbey' and so Sussex himself suggested to

Pyle that he should make a voluntary surrender of Furness; 'which thing so opened to the abbot farely, we found him of a very facile and ready mynde to follow my advice . . .'.

One must not think of Abbot Pyle too harshly for this surrender; heaven only knows what mental anguish he experienced before signing, on April 9th 1537, the deed acknowledging 'misorder and evil rule . . . of the said abbey' and so, 'in discharge of his conscience, giving all into the king's hands'. Pyle realised that the Dissolution would go through, willy-nilly, and by bowing thus to the prevailing political wind he obtained for his monks (and for himself) better provision than was accorded those who continued to oppose the Dissolution. Thus Furness was the first of the larger monasteries to fall. The Abbot received the living of the little town of Dalton, one of his dependencies, reckoned at £40 pounds a year (a good living in those days) while the prior and his 28 brother monks who had signed the abdication received £150 to share between them. The other monks received 40 shillings apiece and a new gown.

The wretched monarch who destroyed the abbey took nothing from the actual fabric of the building but the lead. When at last the roofs fell in and the walls crumbled the abbey was freely pillaged by the local inhabitants for building materials. Many houses in the neighbourhood are constructed out of sandstone blocks from Furness.

Mrs Radcliffe, describing the abbey in 1821, remarked upon the fallen masonry which lay about, the pathless fern and grass through which the visiting tourist had to walk; but today the abbey is devotedly tended and in scrupulous order; one walks about not through grass and fern but over smooth, very green turf.

The church, though roofless and skeletal, is still of extreme beauty; with some concentration one can conjure up a vision of what it must once have been like. The cemetery is gravely garden-like, with a few ancient tombs here and there; but not all of the monks could have been buried here, surely? There is social comment in the determined separation of the monks' quarters from those of the lay-brothers, extending to separate day and night staircases to the church for each group, separate infirmaries, separate latrines. The plumbing of Furness, by the way, is of special interest to serious mediævalists.

The infirmary chapel contains fragments of sculptured masonry and several effigies, assembled from various parts of the abbey. They include the probable figure of an abbot, wearing some rather beautiful drapery, and two tombstone figures removed from the north aisle of the church. Of these one is a twelfth-century, fully armed, cross-knee'd knight, the other, amazingly, is female (of later date, probably fourteenth-century). How this lady, in her kirtle and Plantagenet head-dress, got here in this abbey where no woman was supposed to enter is a matter of great interest, giving rise to much lively expert discussion. She was, it is thought, a distinguished benefactress, brought to the abbey for burial; nonetheless was not this exclusively masculine sanctuary a rather remarkable burial place for a woman? Did old bones stir when she was consigned, dust to dust, ashes to ashes?

There is one other female intruder at Furness; of the two corbels supporting the drip-mould of the great east window of the church one is carved to represent a queen's head; according to some authorities this is Queen Matilda, consort of King Stephen, queried as the other corbel. An opposing school of thought prefers the lady to be Queen Joan of Navarre, wife of Henry IV.

The most interesting effigies on display in the infirmary chapel (although display is too sophisticated a word, for they have simply been carried there and placed on the floor, like dead soldiers fetched from the battlefield and placed in a temporary mortuary) are the two Norman barons in cylindrical flat-topped helmets, vizors down. They lie on their sides, their swords clasped to them, their great shields protectively over their bodies. They are unique in this country; among two of the earliest effigies known here; Norman conquerors who may well have landed at Hastings with William I.

The monks will remain thick around you and dog your steps as you travel northward to Coniston; they had a fishery here, the right to keep a small boat and 20 nets on Thurstainwater, as Coniston Lake was then called (later becoming Thorston Water, which it remained until early in the last century). Baddeley thinks that Coniston is, for the tourist, above all associated with the name of Ruskin, but for the tourist today it is, I should think, rather more associated with the name of Campbell, for it was on this lake that world water speeds were set up first by Sir Malcolm Campbell and later by his son Donald.

The fells of the western shore of the lake are dominated by Coniston

Old Man; named, according to some, for the cairn or 'man' on his summit, while according to other authorities he is named after the Old Men or miners who have, over the centuries, toiled within his bowels. This latter I would suppose the more likely explanation. The Old Man is certainly worthy of his name; a fine mountain and indisputable monarch of this part of the District.

The eastern shore of the lake is flattish, verdant and largely composed of what was once deer-park. This neighbourhood, between the years of 1346 and 1363, was terrorised by a famous gang of outlaws under one Adam of Beaumont. The gang may have had a hide-out on Peel Island, placid as that is now.

Brantwood, Ruskin's home, lies on the eastern margin of the lake, towards its head, below Monk Coniston Moor. Of Ruskin one should say something, for he is more than a mere literary association; the Sage of Brantwood is one of Lakeland's institutions.

He was not Lakeland-born, but had known the District well all his life; his earliest memory, as surely all Keswick visitors know, was of being taken to Friar's Crag on Derwentwater by his nurse. His powers of aesthetic appreciation were developed early; almost too early. His was a lonely childhood, spent with doting and over-anxious parents who encouraged in him complete selfishness and hypochondria. 'I could have wished', he writes in his preface to *The Seven Lamps of Architecture*, 'to have given more examples of our early English Gothic; but I have always found it impossible to work in the cold interiors of our cathedrals. . . . In the course of last summer I undertook a pilgrimage to the English Shrines, and began with Salisbury, where the consequence of a few days' work was a state of weakened health . . .'

The unnatural relationship between himself and his parents, particularly his mother, made it impossible for him to have a normal adult sex-life; he was capable of falling romantically in love but could go no further. He was clearly terrified of sex, fearing that it would in some way imperil him; damage him, take a special something away from him. His reactions to mountains, a few years before his disastrous marriage, had been of the same nature as his reaction to sex; he was enchanted by mountains and loved to think of himself as an intrepid Alpinist—indeed he spoke of himself as such—but in actual fact he only climbed one mountain, the 10,164 feet Buet in the Alps, after which he observed that 'the Alps were, on the whole, best seen from below'.

He would not permit himself to go any further than embraces with his bride, a beautiful Scots girl named Effie Gray; after six years she divorced him since their marriage had never been consummated.

Effie was to say that she could have borne the unnatural physical conditions of her marriage if only Ruskin had not been possessed by an urge to be cruel to her. This urge was undoubtedly encouraged by his parents (who were both pathologically jealous of Effie) but, basically, it was a perverted sexual urge on his part, which became increasingly violent as he became increasingly frustrated by his inability to enjoy his wife normally. The final expression of his sadism came with threats to beat her with a stick, which he made when he learned of her intention to start divorce proceedings against him.

A further complication in the marriage of Ruskin and Effie was that he, presently wishing to be rid of her, did everything he could to throw her in the path of other men so that she should commit an impropriety for which he might divorce her. Effie was scrupulously careful to give him no opportunity. Nevertheless when Millais, the painter, was positively thrust upon her by Ruskin the inevitable occurred; Millais fell in love with the beautiful Effie and Effie returned his feelings. Their behaviour remained exemplary; Ruskin was given no grounds still upon which to divorce Effie; she divorced him.

'Surely such a quiet scoundrel as this man never existed?' asked Millais, in a letter to Effie's mother, discussing the unhappy marriage. One hesitates to call Ruskin a scoundrel; Millais's later, less inflamed appraisal would seem nearer the truth: 'He is an undeniable giant as an author, but a poor weak creature in everything else, bland, and unheartless, and unworthy . . .'[1]

Effie and Millais married; the marriage was a long and happy one. Ruskin, in 1858, about four years after his divorce, fell in love with a child of nine. He continued in love with her; a *Lolita*-like episode, although without the consummation of the *Lolita* story. 'I can't love anybody except my mouse-pet . . . who nibbles me to the very sick-death with weariness to see her', wrote Ruskin. When she reached the age of 18 he proposed to her, but she refused him. He continued to

[1] *The Order of Release.* Ed. by Admiral Sir William James, G.C.B. (John Murray).

propose, she to refuse. She died in her early twenties, leaving Ruskin heartbroken.

In 1878 Ruskin had a first attack of madness, from which he recovered, but after several attacks he went into retirement at Brantwood, which he had bought in 1871. During the next eleven years, until his death in 1900, a few days before his eighty-first birthday he was, except for short periods, virtually insane. It would appear to have been a condition of acute hysteria.

The truth of Ruskin's marriage did not become known until 1947 with the publication of the letters of Effie, Millais and Ruskin,[1] edited by Admiral Sir William James, grandson of Effie and Millais, and released to the world largely as an attempt to clear Effie's name, since most people had tended to feel that a frivolous and unworthy wife must have been responsible for the breakdown of the Ruskin marriage, rather than the author of *The Stones of Venice* and *Modern Painters*.

Ruskin's Lakeland biographers, Canon Rawnsley and Professor Collingwood, made no mention of the tragic truths of his life; it is more than likely that they had never heard of them. The friend they admired, revered almost, could have been nothing but an injured party; genius of his calibre could stoop to nothing petty, let alone squalid. So they wrote of Ruskin as if he were a deity; their biographies leave the actual man shrouded from view, like the Old Man of Coniston upon a cloudy day. Even Ruskin's madness was glossed over.

Ruskin's work has suffered a period of neglect; now it is showing strong signs of coming into vogue again. Ruskin will always be read by some admirers whether he happens to be in fashion or not, for he had the enormous and rare gift of making his readers see things, because he himself saw. His range of vision was limited, clearly he never truly *saw* a human being in his life, but he did see clouds, mountains, buildings, paintings. Of these he wrote, marvellously.

Ruskin bought Brantwood from an artist, W. J. Linton; it was then a small, very picturesque but unpleasantly damp cottage. Ruskin spent thousands upon turning it into a fine house. It is now a centre for the Council of Nature.

W. J. Linton married Miss Eliza Lynn, daughter of a Crossthwaite Church, Keswick, pastor. She became well known under the name of

[1] *The Order of Release.* Ed. by Admiral Sir William James, G.C.B. (John Murray).

E. Lynn Linton as a novelist and she also wrote a very good guide-book to the District, *The Lake Country*, illustrated by her husband and published in 1864. One learns with regret that the Lintons parted, albeit amicably, shortly after they had finished working on the book. Literary projects maritally shared are usually a mistake.

On the western side of the lake, about a mile south of Coniston itself, is Coniston Old Hall, the ancestral home of the Flemings, an important old family locally; you will recall that Stephen's charter to Furness Abbey specified that the monks were to have 'everything within Furness, except the lands of Michael le Fleming'. The Fleming ancestry has been traced back to Reiner le Fleming, Seneschal of William de Meschines, first Lord of Egremont, early in the twelfth century. Sir Thomas le Fleming married an heiress of Sir John de Lancaster and in this way the family came to own Rydal, where they built a second seat. We shall meet the Flemings again when we get to Rydal; for the moment I would only ask you to note the interesting and typical chimneys of Coniston Old Hall, which is now a farmhouse.

Coniston in the old days had no burial-ground of its own; the dead were taken to Ulverston for burial. Near the Old Hall is a place named Jenkin Syke. A *syke* is a ditch and Jenkin was a dead man who was being conveyed in his coffin on a sled to Ulverston. When the burial party reached the village of Torver they looked round and noticed that the coffin was missing; a search back along the way they had come discovered the coffin lying in the syke, having fallen from the sled. Thus Jenkin Syke. I imagine it made a good and humorous story locally for a long time after; the dalesman's attitude to death being straightforward and philosophical.

Torver, to quote Professor Collingwood, is named after Torfi's *ergh* or shieling; Torfi possibly being the same individual as that Thorstein for whom the mere was named.

There is some very good walking round Coniston. The old pack-pony route over Walna Scar to Dunnerdale is an enjoyable one; some seven miles. You can climb up to Goat's Water from the Walna Scar track. Over Goat's Water hangs Dow Crag, one of the finest crags in the entire district, with some good rock-climbing. This is a wild tarn; cold in colour and very deep-looking. You should visit it in stormy weather to get the true essence of it.

There are three tarns on the Old Man range: Goat's Water, Low Water and Levers Water. Low Water, in spite of its name, is the highest, 1,786 feet above sea-level, lying under Buckbarrow Crags just below the Old Man's summit. This tarn is credited with having once been the haunt of the great hairy trout; a creature which sounds apocryphal but need not necessarily have been so. Several of the high tarns are reputed to have been populated by prehistoric breeds of fish well into modern times; I have been told that there is a species of prehistoric fish in Bleaberry Tarn under Buttermere Red Pike, for instance, though personal fishing expeditions up there have so far led to nothing. One should be open-minded upon this question of prehistoric fish; there is the tale of the coelacanth to act as a warning to scoffers. Personally I should never be surprised to hear of all manner of remarkable creatures lurking under the blea waters of the high tarns.

But to return to the pack-pony route over Walna Scar (*scar*, a bare rock) and the way down into Dunnerdale. You might well make a round walk of this, some eleven miles or so, going from the pony-track as it descends Long House Ghyll and taking instead a rising traverse along the fell-side up to the Seathwaite Reservoir; from thence your way would be past the old Seathwaite copper mines to Levers Water and thus back down to Coniston, old mines all the way.

The Walna Scar pony track, on reaching Dunnerdale, crosses Birker Moor to Eskdale, where it picks up the road down Eskdale to the old port of Ravenglass. This was the route used by the pack-ponies to transport ore from the Coniston mines, the ore they yielded being copper and irregular deposits of iron.

The Coniston mines are among the oldest (if not the oldest) and most famous mines in the District; it is believed that mining in the Coniston Fells dates back some 2,000 years. The Romans mined there, certainly; the British tribes most probably did so. The monks mined at Coniston, having many bloomeries there.

Bloomeries, bloomsmithies, are small iron-smelting works dating from the eleventh to the seventeenth centuries; in the seventeenth century larger smelting works came to be built. Coniston was heavily-wooded country (indeed most of the district was heavily wooded with oak, ash, holly, birch and teemed with game in the early days), but by

6 *Furness Abbey: sedilia and piscina in the Presbytery*

the time of the Dissolution the heavy timber had all been felled for iron-smelting in the bloomeries, the wood being burned to procure charcoal to stoke the bloomery fires. The younger trees had been destroyed by the process of bark-peeling for tanning purposes. The dire warnings which modern society receives from time to time for its profligate consumption of natural resources would have been equally applicable, it would seem, to the Furness monks; hewing, peeling and burning away their heritage of forest. Certainly the bare dales of Lakeland today should serve as some warning to us; they were once tree-filled, right up to the base of the crags.

In the Elizabethan era tenants of Hawkshead and Coulton had many of the bloomeries suppressed, in order that 'tops and croppings of the woods might be preserved for their cattle.'[1] The bloomeries, like the mines, first belonged to Furness, then to the Crown and later to private individuals. There are traces of bloomeries to be seen in many places.

I must confess that the old mines and quarries, which to so many people seem a blemish on the landscape, fascinate me. These weathered slag-heaps, these remnants of miners' huts, these dark and chilly entrances of old galleries or tunnels, these fragments of rust-caked metal-cable, old rusted nuts and bolts, drunken winches, twisted truck-rails, piles of slate that slither and clatter as you cross them, blackened bits of metal which protrude, now meaninglessly, from the stone-littered ground, all these are for me imbued with a kind of poetic melancholy; clues to a time past which was important and ringing with noise and is now quite lost.

The standard work on mining in the Lake District is John Postlethwaite's *Mines and Mining in the English Lake District*, first published in 1877 by W. H. Moss and Sons, Whitehaven, and now something of a collector's item. Postlethwaite describes how the mines were worked by a series of horizontal tunnels or levels, as they were usually called, driven along the vein of ore; the ground above and between the levels was afterwards 'stoped' or 'headed' out. If the ore continued downwards, then a shaft was sunk and levels driven from this shaft. The heading process, Postlethwaite tells us, took place thus: '. . . five or six feet of the vein is cut away from the roof of the level, for three or four

[1] E. Lynn Linton, *The Lake Country* (1864).

57

fathoms in length, when strong timbers are fixed across, about three or four feet apart, where the roof of the level originally was; over these, longitudinal timbers are placed, and above these a covering of fragments of rock or vein-stone. This structure is called a "Bunyan" or "Bunnin", and is made sufficiently strong to support the debris which accumulates upon it. As the miner cuts the ground away above, he retains sufficient of the debris beneath his feet to raise him up to his work, and throws the surplus down to the level below, whence it is carried out to the surface. In this way he proceeds until he reaches the level above, after which the whole of the debris upon the bunyan . . . is carried out to the dressing floors, where the ore is separated from the vein-stone and other earthy matter, and made fit for the market.'

When the early miners encountered loose rock they erected oblong timber frames to support the rubble; the level below the frame would then be cleared, another oblong frame would be erected, the area of level below that cleared, and so on. Wooden pumps were used to clear the water which collected in the levels. Before the metal tramways and wagons were used to fetch the ore out of remote parts of the mine wheelbarrows, jackrowls and kibbles were used. Foul air was overcome by artificial air-currents produced by waterfalls; the air-current from the waterfall was conveyed to the miners by an ingenious system of wooden tubes. But the most favoured and easiest method of ventilation was that of simply having more than one opening to the mine.

The working conditions of the early miners especially were extremely exacting; it is not surprising to learn that they were old men in physical fact and not by title alone by the time they had reached the age of 45 or 50.

The ore, in the early days, was washed and dressed by a process of 'tubbing'. Later a system was introduced whereby the ore was dressed over a grate upon which a stream of water fell; the small dirt filtered through the grate, the remainder was passed on to a table and picked over by hand. This job was usually done by boys. In the early nineteenth century, when the Coniston mines were at their peak, several hundred of men and boys were employed there, the mine making returns of from £30,000 to £36,000 a year.

The water for the mining processes was obtained from specially constructed reservoirs. If you search above an old mine you will usually find either a man-made reservoir or a tarn that has been adapted for the purpose of storing and supplying water.

The Coniston copper mines and the Paddy End mines (Paddy End is the oldest working at Coniston) were supplied by Levers Water. The Seathwaite Mines had a reservoir (a converted tarn), the Greenburn mine, below Wetherlam, used a reservoir at the head of the Green-burn Beck.

Until the nineteenth century gunpowder was used for blasting. One unfortunate who didn't get away in time before the explosion occurred was Simon of the famous Simon Nick at the Paddy End workings. It appears that Simon declared that there was a vast treasure of copper ore at a spot where none but he saw signs of a vein. He commenced working there and struck it rich. His mates were deeply envious and to them Simon at last confided that he had been guided to his vein of ore by the fairies. Alas, his secret divulged, the vein of ore vanished without more ado. Simon, vexed with himself for opening his mouth, became careless over his dangerous work and while in the process of making a gunpowder 'nick' blew himself up.

Climbers who use one of the old huts in the Coniston mines as their headquarters firmly believe the place to be haunted. The Old Men (no doubt a wild lot) lived in the huts at the mines during the week, returning to their homes at the week-ends; the climbers now occupy their hut upon an alternative principle, trooping in for a week-end's rock-climbing as the ghosts of the Old Men scurry out; with one exception. He remains, tramps up and down. The climbers are by no means the first people to claim that the Coniston mines are haunted.

Before the invention of gunpowder levels were cut through hard rock by the stope-and-feather method, of which Postlethwaite tells us that the feathers were two thin pieces of iron, about six inches long and half-an-inch broad, flat on one side and round on the other, while the thin, tapering wedge or 'stope' was of the same length and breadth. A hole was bored in the rock and the feathers placed in it, with their flat sides together, parallel with the cleavage of the rock; the point of the stope was then introduced between the feathers and driven in with a hammer until the rock was split. This was a slow, laborious business; the apertures the Old Men thus made were therefore kept as small as possible, not larger than was required to admit one man at a time. If you wander round the old mining areas you will find many of these stope-and-feather-worked mine entrances; about five feet six inches in height and eighteen or twenty inches in width.

Another early method of splitting the rock (although I cannot find mention of it in Postlethwaite) was by heating the rock-face with brushwood; then, when the rock became red-hot, cold water was dashed upon it, thereby cracking the face. Miss Lynn Linton, as well as other authors, mentions this method.

The Coniston mine began to decline in prosperity in 1874 or so; this was partly due to the great depth of the mine, which made it difficult and increasingly uneconomical to work, the low price of copper ore caused by rival overseas deposits, and the substitution of iron ships for wooden ones sheathed in copper. During the years 1877 to 1889 fewer and fewer hands were employed by the mine, until finally scarce a dozen were employed there, where once there had been hundreds. The mine was at last abandoned.

Of these things you may think as you pass the old mines on your way on, and off, the Coniston Fells. Mines are an integral part of the Lake District scenery, an integral part of its history.

Hawkshead was a hunting-ground for the Furness monks. The descendants of the old Viking settlers greatly resented it when Abbot Bankes turned them out of their holdings in order to make himself a deer-park. Just outside Hawkshead, about a half-mile to the north, is Hawkshead Old Hall; the early fifteenth-century Gate House or Court House is where the abbots probably stayed when travelling on circuit, and certainly where they held manorial Courts of Rights. The lower part of this Gate House is now used for farm purposes (perhaps it always was), but on the floor above is a lofty single room extending the length of the building, wholly typical of its period, with an interesting fireplace and a delightful window. You visit the Gate House by asking for the key (and paying a small fee) at the farmhouse across the road.

Near the Old Hall is one of the rather unusual walls one encounters sometimes in these Lancashire fells, made not of dry stones but of flat slabs ranged side by side, quite unlike anything else you will find in the District, and singularly attractive.

Hawkshead itself is the most picturesque town in the District. Wordsworth went to school here, as I suppose everyone knows; you will feel that you should make a pilgrimage to the old grammar school, founded by Archbishop Sandys in 1585, where the poet was a pupil between the years of 1778 and 1783. You will find the visit rewarding, not simply for the name, William Wordsworth, deeply incised in one of the ancient wooden desks, but for the fascination also of deciphering many of the other schoolboy cuttings and carvings, especially on the marvellous old oak window-sills. The earliest carved date I have been able to find is of 1777.

If you are lucky enough to visit the school when it is empty save for yourself and the custodian you may be able to conjure up the imaginary sound of boys' voices together intoning Latin; the sound that this room must most often have heard.

Out of Hawkshead in the opposite direction to the Old Hall lies Esthwaite Water, small, pretty and placid. Past Esthwaite Water lies the village of Near Sawrey, where you should certainly call at Mrs Tabitha Twitchet's house, which Samuel Whiskers thought was his house, which really belonged to Miss Beatrix Potter, who became Mrs Heelis, noted breeder of Herdwick sheep and a devoted friend of the National Trust.

Beyond the village lies the grassy cart-track which Jemima Puddleduck took to the woods where she met the courteous foxy-whiskered gentleman; Mr Todd, no less, or at least a very close relative. Here are the fox-gloves in the glades, the late spring sunshine; if you search long enough I am sure you will find the tumbledown house with the old bucket turned upside-down for a chimney. Further into the wood is just such a wall as Pickles crept behind when he had turned gamekeeper. Everything is here, deliciously and, in a way, astonishingly; just as it was when that hand of genius painted it.

The walk over Claife Heights, which you will find if you follow the cart-track to its logical conclusion, is very pretty, with knobbly country and blue tarns. You will have the Heights almost entirely to yourself, for a car cannot get up there; the cart-track is only for carts and pedestrians (well, tractors and pedestrians, it's probably some time now since a cart went up there); the Heights belong to walkers, birds, foxes and fishermen. Your track goes past Wise E'en Tarn and swings somewhat to the right until it comes to a rather confusing place where two tracks (one of which you are on) cross another track which cuts across at right angles: the two tracks both lead you, ultimately, to High Wray, while if you turn left along the track which cuts across at right angles you will get back to Hawkshead. Turn to your right along this track, instead, and after half-a-mile's walking or so you will see Windermere shining between the trees.

CHAPTER FOUR

Windermere and Ambleside

Mining and sheep are the two traditional staple industries of the Lake District; to these today must be added a third, tourism.

Tourists were drawn to the Lake District, in the first place, through the Romantic Movement. Briefly the Romantic Movement, starting in the mid-eighteenth century and extending until, perhaps, 1845 or thereabouts, was a reaction against the era of Classicism. The Romantics were enormously influenced by liberal forces, by writers such as Rousseau and, later, Godwin, by political movements of liberation of which the French Revolution was the genesis; they were infatuated by notions of Nature, the Noble Savage, the Far Savannahs. Poets dreamt (as did Coleridge) of establishing socialist colonies in virgin countries where they could be free of the restrictions of civilisation and devote their time to philosophy and Back to Nature. Tales of distant exotic lands, of frozen wastes and scorching suns, of peaks and glaciers, strange birds and beasts positively intoxicated the early Romantics; so also did scenes of violence, heroism, nobility, war and massacre, thunder and lightning, castles, knights and ladies, though of course over the massacres an elevating light had to play; readers may recall the celebrated painting by Delacroix, *Scenes of the Massacre at Chios: A Greek Family awaiting Death or Slavery*.

Some of the Romantics were serious artists like Delacroix, or Turner, some were philosophers and poets like Coleridge and Shelley, some were explorers like Franklin and Mungo Park, others were novelists like Scott or Mrs Radcliffe. It is significant that the Romantic Movement not only produced a Scott, but also a Stubbs, with his marvellous anatomical studies.

The Romantic Movement, at first of genuine revolutionary temper, intellectually, politically and artistically, so that the bourgeoisie shied away from it, presently lost its first dangerous cutting-edge and, as movements do, deteriorated into merely being a vogue. Fundamentally staid conservatives like the middle-aged Wordsworth described themselves as *sans-culottes*, Edinburgh society ladies rode in their carriages to see the cellars where Burke and Hare had murdered squalid victims, clergymen panted up mountains and young damsels yearned to dwell gypsy-fashion amidst savage scenery. The most timid suburbanites in Wandsworth and Highbury thrilled at the notion of skeletons in ivied towers, charging scimitar-flourishing Turks, hurricanes and calamities, sights and sounds which, had they been actually encountered, would have induced immediate sweats and palpitations.

The ancient, the gloomy, the blighted, the haunted, the sublime, the picturesque; these enchanted. A stage was reached where a mossy old stone, a mildewy stump, the smallest waterfall, or garden grotto with mirrors set in its recesses to catch the light (I must one day build one of these) gave rise to intense rapture. It should therefore not be difficult to understand why the Lake District suddenly became all the rage: here were mountains, lakes, torrents, rocks, ruined abbeys, clouds, storms, sunsets . . .

Thomas Gray (1716–1771), the poet, is always accredited with having been the first tourist to the Lakes. A timid but nevertheless determined traveller, and honest too (he never wrote about places he had not seen for himself), he set out for the Lake Counties, of which he had heard most picturesque accounts; he was properly equipped, not only with a notebook in which to jot his impressions but also with a small hand-mirror; this an essential for lovers of the romantic, who did not stand to face a view they wished to admire but stood with their backs towards it, manœuvring a mirror in which they attempted to catch a particular frame (to use an apt technical term of the cinema) which would best epitomise the picturesque quality of the scene they were bent upon enjoying.

Gray toured the Lakes indefatigably in spite of the dangers that the District held for travellers (or that he imagined it to hold). His accounts of the scenery sent first a trickle, then a flood of tourists northwards. A steady stream of books about the District now began to appear, too; in 1821 appeared a guide to end all guides, Ackermann's famous publication, *A Picturesque Tour of the English Lakes*, 'Illustrated With Forty-Eight Coloured Views, Drawn by Messrs T. H. Fielding and J. Walton, During a Two Years Residence Among the Lakes.'[1]

It is the illustrations which have made this book so celebrated; few, I suspect, ever read the text. This is a pity, for in the pages of Ackermann one obtains a most lively and faithful view of the Lakers, as they were scornfully called by those persons unable to get to the Lakes themselves. True, we are never shown the actual Lakers direct, but the book is written *for* them, some passages of it are *by* them, and thus, obliquely but how vividly, are these enthusiasts of the picturesque illuminated for us!

Exclaiming, enthusing, they arrived in such numbers, upon the shores of Windermere especially, that there was not room for them all to find accommodation at Ambleside in the height of the season (there was no village then at Windermere, simply a small hamlet named Birthwaite). The Lakers all carried mirrors, of course, and sketchbooks and notebooks with which they would bore their wretched friends when they returned south, just as tourists today bore their friends with home movie-shows of their travels.

Windermere was especially approved of, for the scenery there had everything demanded by lovers of the picturesque: '. . . a bold foreground, a fine transparent sheet of water, with islands, rich woods, and wavy mountains.'[2]

Romantic art had started by imitating what was sublime in Nature, but had now reached such a pitch of the picturesque that Nature was no longer sublime enough and had to imitate romantic art in order to be satisfactory.

There was, of course, terrific opportunity for snobbism in this cult of the picturesque; it was understood that some people had far more taste than others and very scornful were the remarks made by the Tasteful about the Untasteful. One person who was universally acknowledged to have sublime taste was Mrs Radcliffe; to her was given the assignment of writing all the purple passages of Ackermann and splendidly she rose to the task. The absurdity of the fashion she

[1] Title page.
[2] *A Picturesque Tour of the English Lakes.*

followed and then herself led in appreciation of Nature is best revealed, I think, in her comment upon the Vale of Eden, which, she said, wanted 'only a river like the Rhine or the Thames to make it the very finest in England for union of grandeur, beauty and extent'.

The Tasteful, if they cared for their reputations, had to be mindful that they didn't admire the wrong views and, moreover, that they admired them from the right places, or 'stations' as the viewpoints were called. Windermere, Ackermann stated, had five distinctly-featured distant views; these he outlined as, '. . . first, the Langdale-Pikes, as seen between Waterhead and Bowness, and from many delightful stations on both sides of the road; secondly, the views of the islands down the lake, beginning from the high wood-covered grounds, to the north of Skelgill, and ending at a summit, which is very much admired, on the property of the Rev. Mr Fleming, between Rayrigg and Millar Ground; thirdly, the head of the lake, from many situations on the side of the hill between Bowness and Bellman Ground, having the great and lesser islands in the middle, and the Rydal mountains in the extreme distance; fourthly, the view from the Station-house looking over the great island . . .; and fifthly, the Rydal and Ambleside mountains, from many stations between Bellegrange and High Wray, in a combination entirely different from that of the view from Bellman Ground.'

Besides these five major vistas there were many lesser 'sweet pictures and delightful views' to be obtained from numerous stations round the lake. So from station to station scampered the enthusiasts, watchful lest they went into transports of extreme degree over some view which was not, in fact, according to the pronouncements of the pundits, worthy of more than restrained praise.

Very hard indeed were the experts on certain aspects of the Lakes. 'Windermere is, of all the lakes, the only one which is improved by its islands, that add a dignity to its bosom. On the other lakes the islands are prettinesses that do not accord with the character of the scene . . . as the mind does not willingly descend from the grand appearance of nature to her fairy sports.'[1]

But one writer, Clarke, author of *A Survey of the English Lakes*, finally rebelled, condemning 'that cant style of painting which Gilpin and

[1] Ackermann.

some others have introduced into writing. Not a tree, a shrub, or an old wall, but these gentlemen take measure of by the painter's scale; a poor harmless cow can hardly go to drink, but they find fault with a want of grace in her attitude; or a horse drive away the flies with his tail, but these critics immediately find fault with too great quickness of his motions . . .'.

But the Romantics were not the sort of people who could laugh at themselves. To the earthy Clarke they preferred the sensitive Arthur Young who wrote a famous account of Windermere: '. . . what finishes the scene with an elegance too delicious to be imagined, is this beautiful sheet of water being dotted with no less than ten islands . . . all of most bewitching beauty.' The eye met, he said, with 'every picturesque form that can grace landscape with the most exquisite touches of *la belle Nature.*'

Where *la belle Nature* was guilty of omissions hard-headed business-men were present to make good the deficiencies. At Conishead Priory an 'old chapel' was built and an old man was hired to live there as a hermit. One would give much, very much, to be able to have revived the conversation which took place between the ancient and his hirers when they explained to him, or endeavoured to explain to him, what his job was to be.

The tourists of the Picturesque School have vanished (though we shall continue to encounter them in these pages, here and there, as we travel across the District) but something of their mood still hovers about the shores of Windermere; it is a very pretty lake, especially in late April or May, or the first two weeks or so of June before the modern hordes of tourists have arrived, but the prettiness has something slightly artificial about it: Nature has been helped a little too well by lovers of natural beauty. Windermere is rather like a lake in a huge garden; it is not a wild lake, but a semi-domesticated one.

The timid Gray, however, was even able to find Windermere frightening, as Clarke described in his *Survey*:

'At Bowness he was told that the best point of view was on the opposite shore. . . . Curiosity, and a love for natural beauties, were strong incitements on the one hand; but the reflection that there was no convenient way of attaining his desire, unless by crossing the lake in a boat, was a reason almost equally strong for staying where he was.

Being told, however, that not only horses and carriages frequently were ferried over there, but that the common carriers from Kendal to Hawkshead used that conveyance, he ventured to set forward *blind-folded*. He was accordingly landed near Nabgate, had viewed the land-scape, and taken out his mirror in order to view it in miniature, when . . . asking his guide if any persons had ever been lost in crossing the ferry? the Guide told him that about the year 1634, forty-seven passengers were lost . . . by oversetting the boat as they were return-ing from Hawkshead fair. This at once determined Mr Gray not to embark a second time, and he accordingly began to look about for some road to take him to Bowness by land; lifting up his eyes he saw impending precipices on every side (except the lake), a sight as alarm-ing to him as a second voyage; he was so agitated at this prospect, that he trembled for fear, and had just command enough of himself to say to his guide, "Get me to Bowness any way", nor did he utter another word, or ever look up till he arrived there.'

The railway arrived at Windermere in 1847, from Kendal. It was planned to run the line to the lake shore at Low Wood, but Words-worth led a fierce attack on the scheme and the railway was obliged to halt at Birthwaite, below Orrest Head, where a terminus was built and an accompanying village. It should be noted that though Words-worth led a public attack upon the projected railway he privately, and prudently, made enquiries as to whether, if the line were in fact ex-tended to Low Wood, it would be possible for him to purchase shares in the new venture.

The new village was built in a somewhat ecclesiastical style, largely under the influence of the vicar. It is rather odd, this ecclesiastical flavour of the architecture of the many Victorian buildings in this part of the world; ecclesiastical with a touch of Swiss-chalet thrown in. What might be generally termed the Westmorland Lakelovers' Archi-tectural Style. It has even spread, in pockets, to Cumberland; Keswick has a good deal of it, there are odd examples in Borrowdale, a specimen or so in Buttermere.

It may, of course, be a subconscious monkish influence, coupled with an alpine strain naturally arising from the presence of so many mountains. Outside Ambleside, by the way, there is a very pretty and real-looking chalet, while some five miles south-east of Newby

Bridge, at the foot of Windermere, is Cartmel Priory Church, which you should not miss.

All the monks in the District did not, of course, come from Furness. Fountains Abbey had a sheep-farming and wool-industry settlement at Watendlath above Borrowdale. At Lancaster there were Benedictine, Dominican and Franciscan priories. There were two houses of Benedictine nuns in the District also, but as Norman Nicholson nicely points out,[1] the Border Country of the Middle Ages was not the best of places for communities of virgins.

The Augustinians had a priory at Carlisle (of which the cathedral there is a surviving part) and at Conishead and Cartmel too were Augustinian priories. The church at Cartmel Priory has a fascinating history.

At the time of the Dissolution in 1537 the people of Cartmel begged to be allowed to keep the priory church for their place of worship and this request was granted; however, they had no money to maintain the building in a state of repair and when the roof of the main choir collapsed (the choir was the oldest part of the building) they were obliged to leave it fallen. For eighty years this part of the church was open to the skies while the south choir-aisle, enlarged, was used as the parish church (look and you will notice the weathered appearance of those pews that were exposed). Between 1618 and 1623 the church was restored by George Preston of Holker, who also installed the beautiful screens.

Worth noting especially when you visit the church are the Norman arches of the main choir, the Transitional arches of the side aisles, the old stalls in the choir, 13 each side, fascinatingly carved and the tombs of William de Walton, the first prior, and the fourteenth-century Harrington Tomb, with monks chanting a requiem round its base (the Harringtons were a leading local family in early days). When this tomb was opened it was found to contain the bones of a man and, more unexpectedly, a bird; very possibly the deceased's favourite falcon.

The church was damaged by Cromwellian troops in 1643; the wonderful and ancient glass of the east and other windows had been removed to Bowness for safety, where it can now be seen in the east window of St Martin's parish church. It is ranked as some of the finest mediæval glass in Europe.

[1] Norman Nicholson, *Cumberland and Westmorland* (Hale).

The old Gate House of the priory still stands, in Cavendish Street, Cartmel. The upper-floor was used as a grammar school from 1247 to 1790; after that it became a court-room. The grammar school was at first free, but it would only take 20 non-parishioners at a time (lest all the county sent sons for free education). In 1653 a quarterage of six-pence for grammarians and fourpence for petties (small children) was charged; in 1674 the grammarians were being charged eightpence; by 1711 there was a one-and-sixpenny extra charge for Latin and a shilling for English. A tale of rising school-fees, not unknown to parents of today.

Windermere, ten and a half miles long with a width varying from one quarter to one and a quarter miles, is more river in aspect, perhaps, than lake and indeed Baddeley describes it as 'a delightful *river-row* from Lakeside to Newby Bridge'. The steamer trips on the Lake are enjoyable, with a slightly Victorian flavour to them. The deepest water of the lake lies between Ecclerigg and Wray Castle; this castle is of modern origin, built as a late manifestation of the Romantic Mood. Beatrix Potter's father sometimes rented it for family summer holidays. It is now a boarding-school for Merchant Navy radio-officer-cadets.

At the Newby Bridge end of the lake is another building with naval associations; Finsthwaite Tower (now badly neglected), erected in 1799 to celebrate the naval campaigns of that year, when the French fleet suffered its first defeat from Nelson. There is a pretty stroll up to the tower, amongst trees. Beyond are Finsthwaite Heights, with Born-tree and High Dam Tarns; you will find this a pleasant place to amble over.

Another attractive place, curiously ignored by the majority of visitors, is the village of Winster and its surrounding countryside; pastoral, peaceful, at its best in April and May when it is all blossom and lambs. It was at Winster that Jonas Barber, the famous clock-maker, lived 300 years ago. This green vale country behind Cartmel Fell is rich in old manor houses and great family names like Leyburn, Fleming and Barwick. The names of the manor-houses are noteworthy in them-selves; Flodder Hall, Nether Hall, Cowmire Hall (deliciously *Cold Comfort Farm*-ish) and Witherslack Hall amongst them. Witherslack Hall was owned by the Harringtons who forfeited it in 1485 after Richard III, to whom they were loyal, was defeated at the Battle of

Bosworth. The Hall's next owner, Sir Thomas Broughton, was unwise enough to back Lambert Simnel's Rebellion in 1486; for this disloyalty he in his turn was forced to forfeit the Hall. He hid for safety in a cave in Witherslack Woods where apparently he continued to live for several years, his faithful former tenants supplying him with necessities. When at last he died they buried him in the woods and the site of his unmarked grave was pointed out by members of one generation to the next for over 300 years, until memories at last grew vague and finally faded altogether; Sir Thomas Broughton's grave in Witherslack Woods is now lost.

From Winster Vale and Witherslack one should not miss taking in Cartmel Fell church on one's way back to the lake. This church is thought to have been originally a chapel established by the monks of Cartmel Priory. It contains a beautiful window of mediæval glass, as unique and fine as the famous Bowness glass, to which it is indeed related, for it is believed that this Cartmel Fell glass also came from the Priory, brought here for safety from the desecrations of Cromwell's troops. The Five Sacraments depicted in the glass are said to be copies from the Roger van der Weyden triptych at Antwerp. The figure on the left, St Anthony, is English *circa* 1300–1400; he is the patron-saint of basket-makers, charcoal-burners, swineherds and hermits and to him the church is dedicated. The figure of Christ in the Garden, the most unique and striking glass of all, is probably Early English, *circa* 1260, and one of the great church treasures of this country.

At the vicarage (where the keys to the church are available) is kept another treasure; a wooden figure of Christ preserved from the old rood-beam of the church; one of the only two pre-Reformation crucifixion figures now surviving in England.

On your right, as you go back up the lakeside road, is Gummer's How, one of the best of local view points; one which would have enchanted Mrs Radcliffe herself. From it one obtains a marvellous view up the lake. The other view-point you should climb, of course, is Orrest Head, though climb is not exactly the right word for this gentle stroll. The best times for Gummer's How or Orrest Head are before breakfast or in the evening because, either early or late, Windermere is more beautiful than at midday.

Ambleside used to be very picturesque, but (as Ackermann was already complaining in 1821) most of the really old buildings of this little market-town, once famous for its sheep-fairs, have been pulled down. The one really quaint building left is the minute bridge-house over the Stock; an architectural oddity if ever there was. Small as it is it boasts two stories, the upper being reached by an outside staircase. The lower boasts an oven and the oven boasts a chimney. Most authorities agree that it formerly stood in the grounds of Ambleside Hall, a house that has now disappeared and the gardens too; only the former summer-house, straddled over the Stock, remains. Personally I think (but it is entirely my own idea) that this summerhouse was used by a literary dwarf who spent his time in the upper-storey, writing, while some devoted menial (probably his wife) crouched over the oven in the lower-storey making those hot snacks so necessary to authors when in the throes of inspired output.

Ambleside and its neighbourhood are packed with genuine literary associations, but as most of these writers came here solely for peace and quiet we will respect their wishes and let them be.

The Roman fort of Galava in Borrans Field, Waterhead, which Professor Collingwood excavated, is worth a visit, though you should go first to the Armitt Library Museum in Lake Road, where models and diagrams of the site will help you to have a clearer understanding of a place which otherwise you might find rather disappointing. The Romans used this fort of Galava for nearly 300 years; there was an early fort built by Agricola (*circa* A.D. 79) which, being subject to flooding from the lake, was turned into a heightened platform as a site for a second, later, fort, built under Hadrian (*circa* A.D. 122). From Galava a road ran to Ravenglass by way of Little Langdale, Wrynose, Hardknott (where there was another fort) and Eskdale. Another road ran over High Street to Brougham, near Penrith.

Ackermann was mystified by the fort at Ambleside, although he stated that it was thought to be Roman. The Romantics were not very fond of the Romans; one can scarcely visualise a less romantic race than these people who believed in good roads, good baths and good administration. Druids were much more to the fancy of the Romantics. Ackermann turned to Camden, the noted antiquary and historian (1551–1623), who had written of the Ambleside site as 'the dead carcase of an ancient city, with great ruins of walls . . .'. Bricks, small earthen pots or pitchers, small cruets or vials of glass, pieces of Roman money, had sometimes been found there, said the antiquary, together with 'round stones as big as mill-stones . . . of which, laid and couched together, they framed, in old times, their columns . . .'. Nothing of this remained by the time Ackermann's team of writers and artists arrived.

According to Clarke the good people of Ambleside had dug up many pieces of what they called 'free-stone', doubtless Roman relics; these had been 'broken small for scouring-sand, which is a scarce article at Ambleside'.

The Romantic tourists bought potted charr, the delicacy of the District in those days, especially of Windermere; potted charr was dispatched in quantities 'up and down the kingdom'. Nowadays it is tubs of rum-butter. However, if you are looking for something delectable to take home you might visit the potteries at the old Mill beside the Stock; what you find there will not be edible, but it will be something of the District which will give you much pleasure.

Stockghyll Force was the waterfall the Romantics flocked to see, some finding it 'highly awful and picturesque', while Gilpin, suddenly dour, found it instead 'the most unpicturesque we could have'. The truth is that this Force (the local name, together with *spout*, for a waterfall) depends entirely upon the weather for the impression it makes, as indeed do all the waterfalls in the District. After wet, wild weather when the Force is in spate it can be really impressive, but most of the time it is, shall we say, meagre.

The track turning right above the Force will take you on to Wansfell. You might climb the Pike, continue onwards, over and down from Idle Hill to Stock Ghyll on your left and down the ghyll to Ambleside. However you might prefer to pick up the Nanny Lane track on Wansfell that will take you down to Troutbeck, an old village at the foot of the Kirkstone Pass, very attractive, but somewhat too frenetic with traffic most of the time these days. It was here that Thomas Hogarth lived, uncle of William Hogarth.

'Auld Hoggart of Troutbeck' (not to be confused with the Troutbeck of the *John Peel* song, in Cumberland) was born in the village and lived there all his life. He wrote and produced poetic dramas and poems of a bawdy, rollicking nature; there was nothing refined about this

Hogarth who was as honest and vital a poet as his nephew was honest and vital as a painter. The uncle, however, had great talent, the nephew had genius.

'Auld Hoggart's' plays were performed at Moss Gap, Troutbeck, upon a stage of scaffolding; they were entertainments for saints' days and other holidays and were written to divert not wholly uneducated but decidedly robust audiences. Titles ranged from *The Destruction of Troy* to *The Lascivious Queen*; casts were recruited locally. Hogarth had a good knowledge of the classics and, in his more austere moods, enjoyed translating these into simple verse.

He was a spare-time author, writing after supper and on Sunday afternoons. Drinking-songs were his favourite speciality, chiefly about his neighbours; their note was satirical. Despite several minor assaults made upon him by the subjects of these ditties Hogarth did not learn caution until somebody knocked his eye out with a stick (in itself an essentially Hogarthian incident). According to Ackermann this incident made Thomas Hogarth 'cautious not to sing when the parties were present, except he had a good esquire at his back'.

Hogarth's poems were scarcely of a nature to appeal to persons with a taste for the romantically sublime; Ackermann gave his readers a sample of a ballad, but it was a sample designed to show what a coarse individual the poet was. It came from a poem named *The Taming of a Shrew*:

> *The song which I intend to sing, touch women most of all,*
> *Yet loth am I that any here should with me scold or brawl;*
> *For I've enough of that at home, at board and eke at bed,*
> *And once for singing of this song my wife she broke my head.*

No doubt the poet was here interrupted by cheers and laughter. He then continued, describing how the shrewish wife was cured:

> *Now, now, quoth he, the fault I see, she has it from her mother;*
> *It is her teeth infects her tongue, I'm sure it can be no other;*
> *And since, quoth he, the fault I see, whate'er doth me befall,*
> *I'll pull her teeth quite from her head, perhaps her tongue and all.*
> *He took a pair of pinchers strong, and a large tooth pulled out,*
> *And for to pull another, he did quickly set about;*

She then did hold up both her hands, and did for mercy pray,
Protesting that against his will, she'd neither do or say. . . . .

Canon Rawnsley finally made Hogarth's verses acceptable to polite
society by including a selection of them in his *Round the Lake Country*
(although I imagine he was careful over which ones he selected).

If you wish to see in what sort of house Hogarth used to sing his
songs and recite his verses you should visit Townend, a seventeenth-
century yeoman's house, still furnished in the contemporary style. It
is open to the public on weekday afternoons and the National Trust,
who own it, charge admission of a shilling.

The Kirkstone Pass winds upwards from Troutbeck; the part out of
Ambleside used to be called 'The Struggle', an appropriate name in the
old days when pack-ponies, four-in-hands or pedestrians tackled it,
but meaningless in our mechanised era. The old four-in-hand horse-
coaches had many exciting adventures crossing this pass and there is
left us the oft-repeated but still telling comment written in a visitor's-
book by a tourist of those days:

He surely is an arrant ass,
Who pays to ride up Kirkstone Pass,
He'll find in spite of all their talking
He'll have to walk, and pay for walking.

There will be no walking or riding over the Kirkstone in this chapter. We must turn our steps towards Rydal Water and Grasmere,
instead of Patterdale. We have the Lakeland Poets to meet.

CHAPTER FIVE

Rydal and Grasmere

Rydal Water and Grasmere are altogether wilder and indeed more truly romantic than Coniston and Windermere; the fells are craggier and possess more mystery, the dales are deeper, the sky blows over the tops in a constant succession of clouds and clearways, the clouds being heavier than the Windermere clouds and tinged with slight menace. One can believe that among those summits beyond Easedale Tarn or Rydal Fell lie adventures not without danger, surprises and secrets of mountains. The valley bottom, on the other hand, is park-like, vivid with astonishingly green turf and some magnificent old trees, their foliage in late spring and early summer unbelievably rich, especially that of the copper-beeches. The two lakes have gleaming surfaces as though polished daily.

The great house here is, or was, Rydal Hall, hidden among the trees of the Park on your right as you approach Rydal from Ambleside. From the Hall, during the years of the Second World War, there would ride forth on her bicycle a stout and homely Dutch woman, bound for shopping in Ambleside. This was Queen Wilhelmina of the Netherlands, a courageous royalty in dignified temporary exile. It must have interested her to learn that Rydal Hall, some 300 years earlier, had been similarly a retreat in troubled times for Sir Daniel Fleming, whose dignity and personal distinction made him a not unworthy predecessor for the Queen.

The earliest Rydal Hall, second seat of those Flemings of Coniston whom we have already encountered, was said to be so disturbingly haunted that in the sixteenth century the family abandoned it and built a new Hall upon the present site. This new Hall was still nothing more than a simple little manor-house of the period; to it, at the end of the

Parliamentary Wars, the Troubles, came Sir Daniel, who had fought on the Royalist side and was now, as a result, penalised and impoverished by Cromwell's seizure and closure of the formerly Fleming-owned Coniston copper-mines. Sir Daniel had thus decided to retire into the mountains, there to live frugally, waiting for times to change. His physical nourishment in exile was the dalesman's simple diet of oatcake and buttermilk, enlivened by an occasional piece of Herdwick mutton cooked with pot-herbs, but Sir Daniel was exceptionally rich in his intellectual fare, being an enthusiastic antiquary and scholar, so that these years spent in seclusion from the outer world, far from being hard for him, gave him opportunity to pursue his favourite studies and were in all probability the happiest years of his life. From his years of exile at Rydal came the material and notes which later enabled him, in 1671, to write his descriptions of Cumberland and Westmorland which in recent years have been reprinted by the Cumberland and Westmorland Antiquarian and Archeological Society. He was also an indefatigable letter writer and many of these letters are preserved at the Records Office.

After the Restoration Sir Daniel's fortunes changed. The Coniston mines, back in his hands, were reopened; Fleming flourished and became an important man, M.P. for Cockermouth and ultimately a Sheriff of Cumberland. The little Hall at Rydal was enlarged and turned into a fine mansion; frugal living gave way to some opulence of style. Sir Daniel died in 1701; he was succeeded by his son, Sir William, who became a baronet and who in his turn was succeeded by his brother George, a bishop of Carlisle.

Rydal Hall is now a hotel. The Park is the setting of the celebrated annual Sheep Dog Trials and Hound Show.

The celebrations of high-season Grasmere are the old ceremony of Rush-Bearing and the Sports. The Rush-Bearing was formerly an occasion of strewing the church floor with fresh rushes and was performed by adults who were afterwards regaled with ale; now it has become a symbolic festivity in which children, carrying rush and floral emblems and fancies, walk in procession to the church and are later given a tea-party. The Grasmere Rush-Bearing is held on the Saturday nearest August 5th (St Oswald's Day). There is also a Rush-Bearing at Ambleside, held on the last Saturday in July usually.

The famous Grasmere Sports take place on the Thursday nearest August 20th and are attended, at a conservative estimate, by some 10,000 people. The sports include the spectacular guides' race, a fell race up and down Butter Crags near Greenhead Ghyll, in which the contestants ascend and even more startlingly descend the steep fellside in the manner of Gurkhas, placing their speeding feet instinctively as they hurtle down a mountainside upon which the offcome painfully fumbles and stumbles. Another feature of the Sports is the wrestling, Cumberland and Westmorland style, of which it has been said that only the participants really understand what is going on. Hound trails, too, are an important part of the day's programme.

Grasmere is, possibly, the best centre of all from which to tour the District, although one should be warned that in the season it is far from quiet, having long since boomed from a secluded village into a thriving tourist resort. In the town itself there is now nothing of the Lake District proper, except the church. This alone has preserved an indigenous character; its walls have a greenish hue, as of lichen, and like the stones on the fell-sides or the boulders in the beck-bottoms the building seems unchanging and indestructible. It is perhaps the most beautiful church in the District, or at least so it seems to me (I exclude the dale chapels which are in a class of their own), although it would be difficult to analyse the exact quality of this beauty, for it is scarcely strictly architectural. Dedicated to St Oswald, the church can be traced back to the eleventh century with certainty and with less assurance to the seventh century. It was formerly a chapel of the Bellinghams, then of the Flemings, whose tombs are here. The font, by the way, is said to have come from Furness Abbey.

You will notice in the churchyard large numbers of unmarked graves; plain grass-covered mounds devoid of head-stones or memorial tablets of any kind. Until well into the past century it was the custom for the dales people to be buried in unmarked graves; there might seem more dignity in this than in those stone-thronged cemeteries one sees elsewhere.

Grasmere is not only a splendid centre to tour from by car, it also provides pleasurable days for loitering and strolling between the driving. There is the lake to row on; when the weather is fine evening is the best time. The walk round the lake is very pretty; there are also gentle walks along Loughrigg Terrace beside Rydal Water: the walk behind Rydal Mount which takes you under Nab Scar, over White Moss and down into Grasmere at Town End, and, for those prepared for some uphill work, Helm Crag to climb and Silver How to cross. For anyone reasonably fit and not minding a walk that is here and there a little rough an expedition up to Easedale Tarn is worth making.

For keen walkers there is little Codale Tarn lying half-a-mile or so above Easedale Tarn and from Codale Tarn one can walk a further mile across the fell to where Stickle Tarn lies darkly under Pavey Ark, high over Great Langdale. There is the famous way from Grasmere to Borrowdale by High White Stones, Greenup Edge and Greenup Ghyll, returning by the Lang Strath, Stake Pass and the Langdale Pikes. An even bigger round, something in the nature of a good 20 miles, would be to follow the Langstrath Beck up to its source on Esk Hause, then to drop down by Rossett Ghyll (full of moss and young frogs) into Mickleden and thus down Great Langdale to cross the Silver How saddle for Grasmere and home.

This is genuine high, tough fell-walking and you should know how to read a map and use a compass, for it is easy enough to get lost up here in a mist. Wear boots or really stout shoes, warm clothes, including an anorak or wind-breaker of some kind, keep a packet of chocolate or Mint Cake for an emergency ration and have a companion, or companions, with you. Solitary fell-walking is for the old hand and even then carries an element of risk. If you do walk alone, having truly learnt your way around, wear at least one vividly-coloured garment; then, if you do sprain an ankle or break a leg, the search-parties will be able to see you when they come looking. In the old days it was considered loud and ill-bred to wear brightly-coloured clothes on the fells; this silly idea has now virtually died out, except amongst the few remaining stalwarts of the Old Band. There is no virtue whatever in camouflaging yourself to look like a boulder, or a dead sheep. You will only make the business of finding you, should you have an accident, several times more difficult than it need be.

Lastly it is not a bad idea to carry a whistle.

High White Stones is the dome of the *massif* lying to the west of Grasmere; from it you can walk by Gavel Moor to Esk Hause and thus on to the great central hub of the Scafell Pikes. To the north-east of

Grasmere lies the giant Fairfield, sprawling out his limbs: Seat Sandal, Rydal Fell, Scandale Fell and Snarker Pike. To the east lie Hartsop-above-How and St. Sunday Crag. Hart Crag, Dove Crag and Kilnshaw Chimney are the vertebrae of Fairfield, with Lord Crag and Low Pike as the giant's fingertips stretched to dabble in Dunney Beck and Scandale Beck. The more you walk over Fairfield the more devoted to him you will become; he has a very distinct personality. Beyond him, to the north, with Grisedale Tarn between, lies Dollywaggon Pike and beyond her (with a name like that she must be a female giant) looms Helvellyn.

Another long and worthwhile walk from Grasmere would be over Grisedale Hause to the upper reach of Ullswater (a *hause* is a narrow pass), but don't search round here for Grisedale Pike, he is some miles distant in Cumberland.

But for some time now I have noticed that you are becoming restive, reader, and at last I can feel you nudging me, politely but nonetheless with determination. I know what it is. We are at Grasmere, yet not once have I mentioned William Wordsworth. You add that I am making a big mistake if I think you intend visiting Grasmere without ever seeing inside Dove Cottage. Everyone who comes to Grasmere, you say, visits Dove Cottage.

So they do, but the truth is that I wanted you to see something first of Grasmere without William, for these days he has come to swamp all; which is a strange situation considering that few, one suspects, of the thousands who annually visit Dove Cottage ever read his poetry. However all who really know and love the Lake District also love Wordsworth's poems; although when one says that one has to say it with the strongest reservations for, to quote J. K. Stephen's lines:

> *Two voices are there: one is of the deep,*
> *It learns the storm cloud's thunderous melody,*
> *Now roars, now murmurs with the changing sea,*
> *Now bird-like pipes, now closes soft in sleep;*
> *And one is of an old half-witted sheep*
> *Which bleats articulate monotony,*
> *And indicates that two and one are three,*
> *That grass is green, lakes damp, and mountains steep:*
> *And, Wordsworth, both are thine. . . .*

The story of Wordsworth is the tragedy of a two-voiced man.
William Wordsworth first fell in love with Grasmere when he was a
schoolboy at Hawkshead. In the First Book of his uncompleted poem
The Recluse, planned to be a long philosophical poem but in its existing
form merely an autobiographical fragment, written shortly after he and
his sister Dorothy had settled at Dove Cottage, William describes how,

> *Once to the verge of yon steep barrier came*
> *A roving school-boy; what the adventurer's age*
> *Hath now escaped my memory—but the hour,*
> *One of a golden summer holiday*
> *He well remembers, though the year be gone—*
> *Alone and devious from afar he came;*
> *And, with a sudden influx overpowered*
> *At sight of this seclusion, he forgot*
> *His haste, for hasty had his footsteps been*
> *As boyish his pursuits; and sighing said,*
> *'What happy fortune were it here to live!'* . . .

Young William felt that here,

> *Must be his home, this valley be his world* . . .,

and this thought stayed with him, a beautiful ambition that seemed
impossible of fulfilment.

The Wordsworths came of good Penrith stock. William was born
at Cockermouth in 1770, one of a family of five children: Richard,
William, Dorothy, John and Christopher. The family background was
respectable and professional; mainly law and the church. There seem
to have been no poets apart from William. Wordsworth Senior was an
attorney and also agent to Sir James Lowther, later Earl of Lonsdale.
Mr Wordsworth's financial resources were strained, due to debts
owed him by the Earl. In 1778 Mrs Wordsworth died; little Dorothy
was sent to live at Penrith with her grandmother, Richard and William
were sent to Hawkshead Grammar School, boarding in the cottage of
Dame Anne Tyson. The eight years during which William was a schoolboy at Hawkshead were radiantly happy ones for him, although holiday-
times were not so pleasant; Mr Wordsworth followed his wife to the
grave in 1783 when William was 13 and the orphans were left in the

guardianship of their Penrith uncles. 'Uncle Kit (who is our guardian) cares little for us', wrote Dorothy to a friend. She, poor child, had to be at Penrith all the time; a miserable life.

It was while he was at school that William, already a great roamer about the countryside, developed his passionate spontaneous love of the mountains and of nature, a delight wonderfully described in the boy-hood passages of *The Prelude*. He also developed early what might be termed his brilliant reporter's eye; at nine years old, in his first week at school, he saw a drowned man's body pulled from out of Esthwaite Water and was never to forget how, having been sought with grappling irons and long poles:

> *At last, the dead man, 'mid that beauteous scene*
> *Of Trees and hills and water, bolt upright*
> *Rose, with his ghastly face, a spectre shape*
> *Of terror; . . .*

Wordsworth goes on to add (how true an observation and how sound a corrective to those ignorant people who think that violent and horrible sights scare children):

> *. . . yet no soul-debasing fear,*
> *Young as I was, a child not nine years old,*
> *Possessed me, for my inner eye had seen*
> *Such sights before, among the shining streams*
> *Of faery land, the forest of romance.*

The time came for the three oldest Wordsworth boys to leave Hawkshead and dear Dame Tyson: Richard to go to London to become a solicitor, John to go to sea, while William, uncertain whether to go into law or the church, nervous in health, and somewhat of a problem, was finally, in 1787, sent to Cambridge, his uncles no doubt hoping that university would assist him to sort himself out. At Cambridge William, rather surprisingly, emerged as a dandy and a bit of a blade. He was also developing into a conscious poet, for when he returned to Hawkshead for his first and very happy long vacation he took to com-posing verses aloud on his long and lonely walks and in *The Prelude* he gives us an amusing and touching glimpse of himself as he was then;

wandering composing, his companion a Lakeland terrier of long acquaintance, a most tactful and understanding animal, for,

> . . . when at evening on the public way
> I sauntered, like a river murmuring
> And talking to itself when all things else
> Are still, the creature trotted on before;
> Such was his custom; but whene'er he met
> A passenger approaching, he would turn
> To give me timely notice, and straightway,
> Grateful for that admonishment, I hushed
> My voice, composed my gait. . . .[1]

The dog knew only too well what local opinion would be of a young man who went round muttering gibberish to himself and so did Wordsworth. In his later years he clearly gave up caring what people thought; there is the tale told by Hartley Coleridge of how a Grasmere inhabitant who had met the elderly Wordsworth composing verses aloud to himself in a lane later informed the local inn (where Hartley was drinking) that 'Owd Wudsworth had broken out again'.

On this long vacation Wordsworth became convinced that he was to be a poet. Returning to Hawkshead at dawn after a night-long village hop (the Lakeland people have always been enthusiastic dancers) William had a near-mystic experience amongst 'the dews, vapours and melody of birds'.

> My heart was full; I made no vows, but vows
> Were then made for me; bond unknown to me
> Was given, that I should be, else sinning greatly,
> A dedicated Spirit. . . .[1]

Looking back at himself at this moment, 17 years later, in 1805 when the bulk of *The Prelude* was written Wordsworth saw that:

> Strange rendezvous my mind was at that time,
> A parti-coloured show of grave and gay,
> Solid and light, short-sighted and profound;
> Of inconsiderate habits and sedate,
> Consorting in one mansion unreproved.[1]

[1] *The Prelude* (Book Fourth).

A schizophrenic state of affairs that was to last until early middle-age when William's Second Voice, solid, short-sighted and sedate, was to take over and stifle the other William completely.

The Romantic Movement was approaching its climax; in France the Bastille was about to fall. Young William became seized with vague stirrings of revolutionary ardour, he professed himself a *sans-culotte*. He was, in fact, the equivalent of those undergraduates oneself recalls at pre-war parties proffering drinks with the words, 'I can solemnly assure you that this isn't Franco sherry'. Wordsworth, too, had he lived 140-odd years later, would have sat on the pavement outside the Commons agitating for the embargo to be lifted on arms for Spain.

He became restless and instead of applying himself to study, as his younger brother Christopher was to do, in 1790 he spent the long vacation, not reading hard for his Fellowship with a view to going into the church (what an excellent, mealy-mouthed cleric he would ulti-mately have made!) but, throwing caution to the winds, going with Robert Jones, a Welsh fellow undergraduate, on a walking-tour in the Alps; in those days quite a genuinely adventurous undertaking, a scheme regarded by many of his Cambridge friends, he proudly told Dorothy, 'as mad and impracticable'. The tour was great fun, for both Jones and Wordsworth were first-rate walkers. Somehow, in the following January, William scraped through his degree and then went to London, following this, in May, by a walking holiday in North Wales. In September he went up to Cambridge for, it would seem, a final term. In December he departed for France, not to indulge his *sans-culotte* sympathies but for the prosaic reason of improving his French.

He was also supposed to be studying Spanish and, fondly thought his family, had a mind to embark too on Oriental studies; perhaps he might presently, for a while, become a travelling-tutor. Alas for the plans of Dorothy and the uncles in Penrith! France had an inflammable effect on William. At Blois, doubtless in the pursuit of improving his French, William met and soon seduced a 25-year-old French girl named Annette Vallon, getting her with child. Although he professed to be madly in love he did not marry her. Instead he went to Orleans, to Paris; became even more Gallicised and inflammable, carrying the British flag in a Jacobin procession and thereby attracting the interest of Pitt's secret police.

84

His uncles now became alarmed. Whether they as yet knew about Annette is not certain, but even if they did it is reasonable to suppose that as level-headed Englishmen they regarded William's revolutionary activities as far more perturbing than his seduction of a French girl. They shook the family purse-strings at William and early in January 1793, although his daughter Caroline had been born to Annette a mere month previously and he still professed himself to be madly in love, William returned to England, his excuse to Annette being that war was threatening between England and France (it was in fact declared by the French a month later). It seems that he promised Annette that he would return to her as soon as he could; at this stage he still nursed intentions, however ambiguous, of marrying her. On arriving in England he informed his family of his intention to make Annette his wife; his uncles said he would be mad to marry the girl. Although William returned, it is believed, to France in October of that year it seems to have been purely to make clear to Annette that in such troubled times marriage was out of the question; if things became ultimately more settled . . . and so on.

William then went back to England, knowing that he had acted the moral and physical coward. Not only had he been talked by his family out of his allegiance to Annette, he had also betrayed certain definite promises of support that he had given the Girondists. What harsh things these erstwhile comrades had to say to the defecting William we shall never know; he took good care never to repeat them. Desperately ashamed of himself, William's one desire now was to hide. It was, of course, from his own lacerating self-contempt that he wished most to be shielded; such refuge was unattainable. He buried himself in the country with Dorothy; they went first to the Quantocks. Here several influences prompted him to turn to poetry. The first of these influences was Dorothy herself; she, knowing the secret about Annette, though possibly never fully realising the intensity of William's self-disgust, tried to rouse him from his depression:

> *She whispered still that brightness would return,*
> *She, in the midst of all, preserved me still*
> *A Poet. . . .*[1]

[1] *The Prelude* (Book Eleventh).

The second influence was Coleridge. He, at Nether Stowey, was a neighbour of the Wordsworths at Alfoxden. Coleridge was at that time working on *The Rime of the Ancient Mariner*. His talk and companionship stimulated Wordsworth's dormant Muse to activity.

The third influence was Wordsworth's own emotional predicament. He was in that state of great nervous tension, frustrated, sick within himself, which made some kind of emotional release imperative. Any-one with even slight poetic gifts would at that stage have turned to writing verse, especially with Coleridge as a constant companion setting an example; Wordsworth, all incipient genius, was soon obsessively pouring out poems of increasingly miraculous quality. The personal and social circumstances of his writing helped him, almost forced him, to experiment with what was in essence a revolutionary verse-form. Sickened by the lack of courage which had made him drop out of revolutionary activity in France, William not unexpectedly professed himself sickened by the revolutionary movement itself and turned in his reaction to the refuge of contemplating the predicaments of isolated individuals in preference to the chaotic canvas of the social predicament as a whole. As (one suspects) a sop to his own professedly *sans-culotte* sympathies the individuals he chose to contemplate were the poor, the socially humble, outcasts. He had a great predilection for beggars, whom he always depicted in picturesque terms. He enjoyed reflecting upon their solitude, their fortitude, their misfortunes nobly borne, but failed to connect their unhappy lot with its social cause, preferring to extract what he called 'moral truths' from the simple stories of these people.

Wordsworth not only selected simple, humble people to write about, he also experimented endlessly with the technique of a simple style. Many of his greatest poems are so stripped and lean and apparently effortlessly beautiful that one never ceases to marvel at his achieve-ment; the result, of course, of hours and days of intense work.

William and Dorothy were happy in the Quantocks, but it was becoming increasingly difficult to solve the financial problem of how they were going to live. William now knew he wanted to devote him-self wholeheartedly to poetry; poetry did not pay. At this point they went to visit friends at Keswick and there William procured himself a patron; a legitimate thing enough for a creative artist to do. Raisley

Calvert, younger brother of William Calvert of Greta Bank, was dying of tuberculosis and William managed to persuade him to leave a legacy of £600 (which ultimately became £900) to one who one day perhaps would wear 'a wreath of laurel on his brow'.

'I should have been forced by necessity into one of the professions, had not a friend left me £900', the poet was later to confess. 'This bequest was from a young man with whom, though I call him friend, I had but little connexion; and the act was done entirely from a con-fidence on his part that I had power and attainments which might be of some use to mankind.'

With this legacy in his hands William thought of Grasmere. At last he might realise his boyhood ambition of living in that secluded and beautiful place. By a stroke of fortune Dove Cottage, previously a small inn, was available as a future home for himself and Dorothy. In *The Recluse* he gives excited and happy exclamations of triumph:

> *And now 'tis mine, perchance for life, dear Vale*
> *Beloved Grasmere (let the wandering streams*
> *Take up, the cloud-capt hills repeat, the Name)*
> *One of thy lowly dwellings is my Home. . . .*

Anyone who has ever achieved a childhood's dream-house of their own (and I confess myself to being one of these lucky people) can understand the poet's delight in Dove Cottage and Grasmere (Gras-mere as it was then). The very stones of the house, the clouds sailing down the valley, the sheep calling on the fell, were sufficient to enchant him. The very act of opening the window on a rainy day and smelling the wet air was intoxicating. But even in these days of happiness in his new home William's guilt was never far away and he was constantly brooding upon the cost of this dream-like existence, a cost, he felt, of,

> *. . . the realities of life so cold,*
> *So cowardly, so ready to betray,*
> *So stinted in the measure of their grace. . . .*[1]

Excuses for himself were forever wriggling in his brain, like worms, but he could not successfully smother words like 'cowardly' and 'betray'; his conscience daily seared him, a flame he could not extinguish. He

[1] *The Recluse.*

told himself desperately, 'On Nature's invitation do I come, by Reason sanctioned'. In spite of the sanctioning of Reason his heart still told him that he should have been elsewhere. The vision of Annette, even more reproachfully the vision of his daughter Caroline, rose constantly before him; he thought too of his former comrades in France, many of whom were now dead. If he had stayed to march with them as he had said he would he might now be dead himself. He had ducked the issue that they had faced, misguided as that issue might have been. He tried to divert his attention to more soothing subjects, especially reminding himself that he had at last provided a real home for his sister Dorothy:

Ay, think on that, my heart, and cease to stir. . . .[1]

How he longed for his miserable heart to cease stirring! Oh to be shut away, in every sense, from the pressing outside world that had broken him, safe from memories:

Embrace me then, ye Hills, and close me in. . . .[1]

An anguished cry.

William and Dorothy arrived at Dove Cottage a few days before Christmas of 1799. By the spring they both felt that '. . . this Vale so beautiful begins to love us.'[1] Dorothy was happier than she had ever been in her life before, spilling out her joy in the Journal that is her equivalent of William's poems of that period. She worked about her treasure of a new home, began making a garden, went for daily walks, very often with William, hunting mosses, flowers, views and waterfalls. Her brother worked, walked, gardened, did jobs round the house (in one Journal entry Dorothy tells us that William had just cleared the snow from the path to the necessary) and saw a good deal of Coleridge who had come to live with his own family at Keswick. This was William's great period as a poet; miraculous verse seemed to pour out of him. He was, in fact, in love again; with Grasmere and with his sister Dorothy.

On William's behalf it must be stressed that Dorothy was now acting as an inspiration to his poetry writing and he was in love with her as a poet is in love with his Muse; on his side there was a certain amount of

[1] *The Recluse.*

fantasy in this near-incestuous relationship, he wrote of her as Lucy, not as Dorothy. Dorothy, on the other hand, was head-over-heels in love with William; attentive reading of the Journal makes this clear. Here she is writing on March 4th 1802 about William's absence from home for a few days; she cannot bear being without him, but decides to put a brave face on the separation: 'I *will* be busy. I *will* look well, and be well when he comes back to me. O the Darling! Here is one of his bitten apples. I can hardly find in my heart to throw it into the fire. . . .'

We read of long, affectionate midnight conversations, of pettings on the carpet before the fire when William was tired, of the day they lay together in a ditch imagining that this silent sympathy was what it would be like when they were dead and buried near each other. It is true that they were each in their greatest phase as creative writers and that creative talent carries with it a certain amount of abnormality (as well as sick-headaches and stomach upsets, with which both brother and sister were frequently afflicted), but there seems to have been more to their relationship than exceptional sympathy and sensibility. The Journal describes life at Dove Cottage as the life of two lovers, physically unconsummated as that love in all likelihood was. They were very secretive people; the truth of William's affair with Annette did not become known until some 60 years after his death. What other secrets were there to hide? One can only guess. Perhaps none. Perhaps many.

Three years of this poetically marvellous and distinctly unusual *ménage* slipped by; Dorothy kept her Journal, perfected the garden with Coleridge's help over a bower and a seat, baked bread and pies, starched and clapped the small linen, visited friends and entertained them in her turn, copied William's poems for him, ready to be sent to his publisher. His first volume of verse, *Lyrical Ballads*, with which Coleridge had collaborated, had brought Wordsworth no money, some admiring recognition from the few, and considerable abuse and ridicule from the many. His poems were in advance of the taste of the time. He was now working upon a second edition of *Lyrical Ballads*, for which he wrote his celebrated critical Preface.

With Dorothy doting on him, Coleridge admiring him and his poems winning him increasing attention Wordsworth's self-esteem began gradually to re-establish itself. None but his closest relative knew anything of his unfortunate past, everyone else took the author of *Lyrical Ballads* at his poetical face-value; a man who invariably produced a moral at the end of each poem must himself be a man of high moral integrity. Wordsworth had now reached a point, of course, where, had he been capable of it, he could have displayed a newly gained personal integrity, but such a quality was not genuinely within him. One would have expected, at least have hoped, that he would at all events have come clean, so to speak, with Coleridge; at that time a very intimate friend who touchingly made no secret with the Wordsworths of his own unhappy marriage, failures and weaknesses. To him Wordsworth, if equally honest, should have confided. Wordsworth did not so confide; instead his attitude towards Coleridge became increasingly smug and condescending.

Worse still, Wordsworth was becoming irked by Dorothy's close proximity. Their life was conducted at such a pitch of sympathy that it was as if they were always naked together. At first William had needed this closeness; it had helped him, had enormously reassured him. To have Dorothy always at hand, always full of understanding had been a necessity to him in his years of self-reproach and torture. Now, as he began to feel stronger, such support was no longer desirable. Grasmere and Dove Cottage had healed him to the point where he could successfully stifle his traumatic memories; stuffing them down into his subconscious mind, instead of having them forever searing his immediate consciousness. Dorothy was a sole sharp reminder of his sufferings; she had shared some of his anguish of mind, on his behalf, and this made her unwelcome now that the anguish of mind had abated.

Was there, too, a lurking suspicion in his heart that some of his new literary admirers would find life at Dove Cottage somehow not quite respectable? William, who had thought so badly of himself, wanted desperately to be thought of highly, and by the best people withal. Sir Walter Scott spoke of visiting; perhaps his publisher would come. Was sister Dorothy not rather over-intense, too passionately adoring, eccentric, to be a wholly suitable hostess for distinguished visitors?

Among the friends of the Wordsworths were two sisters; Sara and Mary Hutchinson. The unhappily-married Coleridge was miserably in love with Sara; Wordsworth found himself vaguely attracted to Mary. A plump, plain, placid, incredibly good-natured young woman, untalkative and not particularly intelligent, she made a soothingly restful change from Dorothy. William began to see more and more of Mary Hutchinson. Finally they became engaged. Dorothy wrote in her Journal that she felt the threads snapping about her heart.

Yet so much of William's double-personality remained that, on the very night after his betrothal, on his way back to Dorothy and Grasmere, he wrote for Dorothy, to Dorothy, what was probably the most beautiful of all his Lucy lyrics; 'Among all lovely things my Love had been . . .'. This is a love poem, and a deeply sincere one. He was also to write one in due course to Mary, 'She was a Phantom of Delight . . .', but in this he quickly found himself describing the poor girl as,

> *A Creature not too bright or good*
> *For human nature's daily food. . . .*

In short Dorothy, a heady stimulant, had been over-rich for William's digestion and he was turning, in an effort to avoid dyspepsia, to a plain bread-and-butter diet.

William and Dorothy now travelled briefly to France together to meet Annette and explain things. Then they returned to England, their mealy-mouthed expedition safely accomplished, and within a week William and Mary were married. Dorothy, of course, was with them. The trio, immediately the breakfast was eaten, set out on the journey to Grasmere. The wedding-night was spent at an inn near Helmsley; Dorothy and William took an evening walk together to look at the ruined castle there, leaving Mary alone in the kitchen of the inn.

So Mary became installed at Dove Cottage. Dorothy's Journal-writing soon dwindled, then stopped altogether. She had no heart for it now that there was another to read it besides William. As for William, he presents to us a tragic, extraordinary, but not unknown phenomenon. He had seemed to be recovering from his guilt-complex, but in fact he had been burying it deeper and deeper within himself where it had continued to wrack him in a way far more dangerous than when it had been nearer his surface-nerves. Finally, unable to bear the gnawing anguish any longer, William, to all intents and purposes, committed suicide. His marriage to Mary was death to him as a poet;

he embraced her knowing what she would do to him; he wanted it done. Plump, placid, gormless Mary overlaid William the poet, quietly asphyxiating him. William had wanted it that way.

Of course he continued to write verse; tedious, pretentious stuff that the public (which, generally speaking, hates real poetry) took to its bosom with enthusiasm; this new, profound, mature Wordsworth was infinitely preferable to the green young Wordsworth who had written *Lyrical Ballads*. In *The Prelude* William recaptured some marvellous boyhood passages, then relapsed into his Second Voice, the old, fly-blown sheep bleating on the fellside on a jaded August day, and with this Voice he sang henceforth, with one or two exceptions. As Matthew Arnold was to remark, Wordsworth himself seemed to have had no idea that the bulk of his later work was entirely without merit; indeed the poet often remarked that his later work was much superior to his earlier verse. 'More profound poems of my later years', he said. But William had joined the ranks of the living-dead and the living-dead are not self-critical.

The public increasingly lionised Wordsworth; everyone came to Dove Cottage. For a picture of the cottage *ménage* in its closing years one should read De Quincey's brilliant *Recollections of the Lakeland Poets*. Wordsworth he found to be a tall, ruddy-faced man with grizzled hair and a cordial manner. Mrs Wordsworth came as a bit of shock; De Quincey, like all the other lionising visitors, supposed that this was the love of the poet's life, not realising that this was a cosy cushion, a soft pillow, obtained to rest with after the turbulence of an affair with a French girl of whom nobody had heard hint or whisper and passionate attachment to Miss Dorothy Wordsworth, the brown-faced, jerky, near-hysterical woman who followed Mrs Wordsworth into the room: for indeed the inhibited and frustrating life Dorothy now led had flung her into a state of mounting hysteria which was ultimately to become a form of insanity.

De Quincey became very friendly with the Wordsworths, although there were faults on both sides which ultimately destroyed the friendship. The most revealing observation that De Quincey made about Wordsworth (among many) was that he, on one occasion, cut the pages of a new volume of poetry with a buttery knife.

Shortly after this first meeting with De Quincey, the Wordsworths

8–10 WORDSWORTHIANA: *Dove Cottage; Grasmere Church; the Wordsworth graves*

1 (above) *Great Langdale and the Pikes,
from Silver Howe, near Grasmere*

12   *High Bridgend Farm, and the slopes of Helvellyn*

moved from Dove Cottage, desiring something larger now that there were children in the family (and growing crowds of visitors). De Quincey rented the cottage for many years, using it as a repository for his large collection of books once he himself had moved away. The Wordsworths (to whom the Lowther family had at last paid the money so long owed) lived first at Allan Bank, after leaving Dove Cottage, then at the Rectory, finally at Rydal Mount, the poet's home from 1813 until his death in 1850. More and more people flocked to Grasmere, attracted by the fame of Wordsworth; he professed to be greatly annoyed by this intrusion of his sanctuary, but one cannot write enthusiastically of a place and then expect one's readers not to come flocking. In fact Wordsworth greatly enjoyed publicity and since publicity meant hordes of sightseers there was no alternative to a crowded and spoilt Grasmere. The formerly secluded vale became busier and noisier year by year, Wordsworth became more and more esteemed until he was finally made Poet Laureate. Dorothy became increasingly demented.

Thousands of people now visit Dove Cottage each year, but nothing is there now of the Wordsworths, save perhaps the faintest aroma of Dorothy in the little back-kitchen where she once happily baked, or starched the small linen. Too many people have trooped through those rooms, gaped and gawked. The nearby museum, on the other hand, is very well worth a visit; it contains manuscripts of William's poems, Dorothy's original Journals, interesting letters of De Quincey and splendid ones of Coleridge. There is a mask (death-mask?) of Wordsworth; big-nosed, long-faced, loose and clumsy-lipped: one would give a great deal to have seen him as a youth, walking the Lancashire fells with his Lakeland terrier, before guilt and smug success had in their turn placed their prints upon him. There is a delightful and touching sketch of Wordsworth and Hartley Coleridge, in back-view, walking together; Wordsworth immensely tall and thin, Hartley a little child-man, waifish and pathetic.

The graves in the churchyard lie in a corner together; William and Mary, Dorothy, the Wordsworth children who died young, Dora, the poet's daughter who died in adult life, little Hartley in a large, ornate tomb which is immensely unsuitable for one so small and natural, some of the Wordsworth friends. Samuel Taylor Coleridge himself lies

97

buried in Highgate; far away. One can spend long in this corner of Grasmere churchyard, supposing that you choose a quiet time to go there, in autumn or winter. Yet these are but graves, they house the dead; for some living essence of the people buried there one must turn to Dorothy's Journals, William's poems, old letters written on yellowed paper in faded ink.

CHAPTER SIX

The Langdales and Eskdale

All the time we are drawing closer to the central *massif* of this country; the great hub of the wheel of mountains, as Wordsworth described it in his much-quoted but never to be improved upon phrase. This great hub consists of Scafell and his Pikes, with the wheel-spokes formed by surrounding ranges; Great Gable, Kirk Fell, Pillar and Steeple to the north-west, Brandreth and the Buttermere Fells east of these, to their east again Fleetwith, High Scawdel, Dalehead, Hindscarth, Robinson; the sublime main ridge of the Newlands Fells, with High Scawdel swinging into a tributary ridge of Maiden Moor and Catbells. Directly to the east of the Scafell Pikes lies Great End, with Allen Crags, Glaramara (lovely as the name) and Rosthwaite, or Chapel, Fell. To their east are Gavel Moore, Langdale Combe and High White Stones, Greenup, Ullscarf, Coldbarrow Fell, Armboth Fell, High Seat and Castlerigg Fell (a lengthy spoke of the wheel, this). To the south of the Pikes are Esk Pike, Bow Fell, Crinkle Crags and Stonesty Pike, with Cold Pike and Pike o' Blisco swerving to the east as a nab, or nose, thrusting between the two Langdales. Beyond the Three Shire Stone on Wrynose are Wetherlam, the Seathwaite and Coniston Fells, while dipping southwards from Lingcove Beck below Bowfell (which may be written either as two words or one) runs the long, lean range of Black Crag, Hard Knott, Harter Fell, Birker Moor, Birker Fell, Ulpha Fell and Great Worm Crag. When you really know the District you will be able to stand at any given point and name the names, in the way a school-master names his class, or a huntsman his hounds. You will also enjoy the warm, familiar feeling that comes from being surrounded by friends, albeit friends who have to be accorded constant respect.

The Langdales, Great and Little, lead you from Grasmere towards the central *massif*. This is scenery which Wordsworth himself often explored and wrote about in prose more deathless than much of his verse. The scenery, as you penetrate further and further in to the high places, becomes wilder, the daleheads more lonely, the crags more authoritative and precipitous. Clouds swirl lower, sheep cry and ravens croak; you will never be far from the sound of a beck running. When the Wordsworths came to the District to live at Dove Cottage 'the lordly birds of the air', as William called them, still included eagles; of these more will be said, later. Now you will see, besides ravens, buzzards and occasional kites. The former mew so plaintively as they circle aloft that you will be inclined for a moment to search for a kitten in the sky. A buzzard is so large and wheels so impressively overhead that one can be forgiven if, at first glance, one takes the bird for an eagle; the mewing-cry and broad, blunt-tipped wings, like the wings of a giant moth, will correct the impression. On the ground the bird has the sidelong, waddling hop peculiar to the eagle family. Although generally feared by smaller birds and little animals upon which it preys, the buzzard (and I suppose this goes for others of his family too) shares the peculiarity of lions and tigers that his victims know when he is merely out for a stroll and when he means business. There are occasions when I hear a buzzard calling and on going outside to look discover the chickens scampering for shelter like wartime citizens hearing an air-raid alert; meantime the little wild birds shrink into the bushes, chattering warnings. Suddenly, then, the garden and hedges become very quiet, while the killer aloft circles round and round, keenly scanning the landscape below. Buzzards often hunt in pairs; they seem to converse together as they prowl. Whether it is the female bird, like the lioness, who does the bulk of the hunting I don't know; she is larger than the male bird by some two inches.

I once watched, from High Scawdel, a buzzard chasing a lapwing; the poor bird exclaimed plaintively as he swooped and swept to evade his pursuer; the outcome of the chase was lost to me as they whirled away over Steel Fell.

But on those occasions when the buzzard is, so to speak, merely out for a saunter the chickens in the farm-fields continue their pecking

and scraping without a tremor, while the little garden and hedgerow birds giggle with each other about the bogeyman flapping overhead. One morning I saw a small bird merrily swooping and darting about a buzzard, obviously teasing him. The buzzard ignored the impertinent rascal, but presently the teaser went too far, whereat the buzzard turned on him with a kind of token swoop and the little bird (but still laughingly) dived in a rush down to his friends below, who greeted him with an admiring and much-amused chorus.

The really thrilling sight (and sound) is of ravens tumbling and chasing one another in sport above the fells; as they race down the wind you can hear the air brushing against their wings with the sound of tearing paper. This you will often hear if you walk alone, or if in company then quietly.

Great Langdale, although very popular with tourists, is still in its best parts the province of sheep-farmers and rock-climbers. Wall End is the famous sheep-farm hereabouts; it also has a celebrated barn in which many a climber has found refuge. Gimmer Crag is the great climbing-place in Langdale. Pavey Ark and Stickle Tarn are fine and wild if you struggle up to them above Dungeon Ghyll; Pavey Ark has several good rock climbs and one nice little so-called walk across its face, Jack's Rake; a *rake* being a narrow passage, usually a narrow ledge, across or through crag. Jack was a very agile Stone Age man who used to come up here collecting flints.

Above Wall End lie the twin dale heads of Mickleden and Oxendale, divided by Stool End. In Mickleden are the remains of a Bronze Age settlement. From Oxendale you can ascend Hell Ghyll to Bowfell, while Mickleden leads you to an old sheepfold where you can either branch right, under Black Crags for Langdale Combe and the Stake, or left up Rossett Ghyll for Hanging Knott, Angle Tarn and Esk Hause. This is country I know well, yet I think I can honestly say that I have never seen either Mickleden or Oxendale, Rossett Ghyll or Hanging Knott in sunshine, except, perhaps, for a few stray and watery gleams at the tail-end of a rain storm. In my mind's eye all here is murky and thick with rain, sepia and pewter-coloured, with blea patches in the dale bottoms; in short I have only been here in clarty weather, as the local expression goes. Angle Tarn, for me, is a pewter mirror-back flashing through straying curtains and puffs of cloud;

when the margin of the tarn is reached one discovers a sad little stretch of water lapping in small voices against stones.

It was here, going up Esk Hause from the tarn, walking alone in heavy mist, that I once met what I thought was a yak. The beast gave me a nasty shock. Quakingly I made closer inspection and found it to be a sheep, enlarged out of all proportion by the optical illusion of the mist. In this manner one also, from time to time, encounters bears upon the fells, looming on all-fours; dark and shaggy. One drizzly evening a party of us thought we were being approached by an elephant; this, however, was two young neighbours, mooching up the track, lovingly entwined with a loose anorak sleeve dangling in front of them like a trunk.

Crinkle Crags, a good afternoon's fun, should be explored from either Oxendale or Lingcove Beck; these crags are exactly what the name says. Lump after lump of crag appears as you wander over this top; the lumps interspersed by smooth slabs of so-called boiler-plating, set at angles on which, if you walk unwarily, you will skid. After rain the crags hold many minute tarns, which I suppose the unromantic would describe as puddles. The estimated number of lumps, or knobs, on Crinkle Crags varies with each person who counts them.

Little Langdale is much milder than Great Langdale. Little Langdale Tarn and Blea Tarn are low-lying and gentle, like the larger, reed-whispering Elter Water. From Little Langdale starts the Wrynose Pass, locally pronounced Ráynus; in the thirteenth and fourteenth centuries it was called Wreneshals, Wrenhalse or Wreneshalse, Collingwood tells us, from *hals*, the old Norse for *hause*, hause being as we have already discovered a pass. But the Wrenes part of the name remains a mystery; who or what Wrenes was will possibly never be known. Certainly the name of this pass has nothing to do with a nose, wry or otherwise.

This District was once a great place for smugglers and moonshiners. Of the moonshiners the most notorious was one Lanty Slee, of Irish descent although his birthplace was Borrowdale. He lived, a century ago now, at Low Arnside, between Skelwith Bridge (pronounced Skellyth) and Coniston. Here, it is said, he had a still in his stable. However, since the authorities were always after him, he had several other stills cunningly concealed about the neighbouring fells. One

The Langdales and Eskdale

was in Bessycrag Quarry, overlooking Little Langdale Tarn. A convenient spring formed a small tank which was connected to his condenser, or 'worm'; the whisky he made (said to be excellent) was kept in a tiny secret cellar there. Slee was arrested several times and gaoled in Ambleside. There is still in existence a newspaper account of one occasion when he stood trial, in 1853; his appearances in court were greeted with enthusiasm for he had a good Irish wit on him and could be relied upon for entertainment, even when performing from the dock. He died in 1878, aged seventy-eight, at Greenbank Farm.

The pass over Wrynose and Hard Knott, down into Eskdale and thence to the formerly busy port of Ravenglass (in the first place a Roman port) was a Roman way. The Romans, when they arrived, divided the area into districts, each district held by a fort. Each of these forts carried a garrison of 500 or 800 men and if trouble broke out could call upon the legions for help; the legions were quartered at Chester and York. Communication was by a highly organised and efficient system of runners. Lines of communication were the main north-western road from Ribchester to Carlisle, with a parallel road through Lancaster and Kendal. From Carlisle there was a road to the Northumberland coast and to the line of forts along the southern shore of the Solway. Another route came direct from Ambleside over High Street to Brougham, as we have already seen, while beyond Ambleside went the road you are now travelling, by Wrynose and Hard Knott to Eskdale and Ravenglass. At Hard Knott was a fort.

This Hard Knott fort, or Hardknott Castle as it is frequently called, lies below Border End, on your right as you descend by the pass into Eskdale. It is a lonely place, especially wild and impressive at sunset when the purple ridges of fells and clouds are slowly devoured by the dusk which rises from the dale bottom and the landscape becomes, most convincingly, a place for Brigantes and wolves. The fort, some 2,000 years old, has been carefully excavated; the imaginative will find it an exciting place. The fort was probably built by one of the Agricolas in the first century; it was garrisoned for some 300 years, then probably abandoned in the reign of the Emperor Hadrian, who eased the difficulties of occupying this part of the country by building his famous wall. It is thought that after the fort ceased to function in its original capacity it continued to be used, in part, as a rest-house.

The main fort was 250 feet square; enclosed by a deep ditch with a gateway in each side and a watchtower at every corner. Inside the fort were barrack blocks, a headquarters, the regimental chapel, the commanding-officer's house and offices, and granaries. 250 yards to the north-east of the fort lies the parade-ground, while to the south-east of the fort were the soldiers' baths with cold, warm and hot rooms and dry-heat; bathing accommodation much in advance, so to speak, of that enjoyed by armies today. A small circular building, which may have been a temple, adjoined the bath-house and there was also in all likelihood a soldiers' wayside tavern. This place, of course, was garrisoned by soldiers who were not Roman-born, but conscripts of European peasant stock.

Under Roman occupation the Brigantes became comparatively civilised; they developed an agriculture and were trained to become legionaries themselves in time. Trading centres grew and flourished, at Carlisle for instance, while thriving settlements came into being near the larger forts. After the Romans left their civilisation survived for a long time; but gradually, over the years, it declined and finally disappeared.

At Ravenglass is another Roman bath-house known as *Walls Castle*; the best-preserved Roman building in the north of England. This bath-house was some 50 feet long by 40 feet wide and the remains now reveal two rooms and a part of two others. But we have not arrived at Ravenglass yet, we are still upon Hard Knott, staring before us into Upper Eskdale while behind us is the steep and twisting road down which we have come.

During the great days of the wool-trade long strings of pack-ponies used this road; the animals hung with bells, which jangled and rang in rhythm with the clattering hooves. One would give much to be able to recapture the sound of a pack-pony train. Travellers on horseback, we are told, started out early in the morning to avoid the pack-trains, which were very difficult to pass.

These were the legitimate pack-trains, travelling by day. At night came other pack-trains, in very different style; silently, without bells, the ponies' hooves muffled with straw-bindings, for these were the enterprises of smugglers. The Wrynose–Hard Knott pass was, in particular, a much-used smuggling route and many were the skirmishes which took place about the Three Shire Stone between smugglers and excise-men.

The little and independent Isle of Man could import wines, spirits, tobacco, tea and lace without duty. Around the year of 1670 some enterprising Lancashire settlers went there, encouraged foreign trade and resold to local smugglers, who organised a running-trade to the Solway Firth. They used small boats, or 20-gunned luggers. This trade was in its heyday in the late eighteenth and early nineteenth centuries, thriving at the little local havens of Drigg, Seascale, Sellafield, St Bees. The Revenue people tried to counter it with a cutter harboured at Whitehaven and sloops from Annan and Silloth.

As in Cornwall in the smuggling days the District rejoiced in several notorious smugglers' houses, or more correctly, meeting-places, where the cellars were stocked with illicit liquor. Neb Cottage, at Seascale, was a famous smugglers' alehouse, while beside the Gosforth–Holmrook road there formerly stood a cottage known as Mary Larg's which was also a smugglers' haunt; a considerable cache of smuggled goods was kept there. Mary, the story goes, came to a not unexpected end on the local gallows-hill, convicted of smuggling. The cottage has long since been pulled down but the place where it stood is called Marylands, a clear derivative of the old name. Some years back the former cache-hold was discovered by a farmer.

At Fell Foot in Little Langdale, about a mile up the Wrynose road above Little Langdale Tarn, is an old farmhouse with the arms of Fletcher Fleming over the door. This was formerly a well-known smuggling house. Behind it we meet not smugglers but Norsemen, for there is an odd terraced knoll which may not appear much to the casual eye but which Collingwood believed to be a Viking Thing, or parliament-mount, similar to the Tynwald Hill in the Isle of Man. If such were the case then Fell Foot was the political centre, so to speak, of the Icelandic colony; an important place.

Eskdale is topographically divided into the Upper and the Lower; it can also be divided into what might be termed a public dale and a private dale. There is no lake here and car-bound tourists can do little more than stick to the main road, gleaning what meagre knowledge they can of Eskdale as they drive westwards to Ravenglass or Gosforth. Eskdale is a wonderful part of the District, one of the very best, but it can only be truly discovered by pedestrians. To the motorist it remains virtually inaccessible.

What will you, if car-bound, see of Eskdale as you drive down it? Of Upper Eskdale, uninhabited and moraine-scattered, nothing; roads do not touch it. You will continue down to the central reach of Eskdale where hidden Upper has given way to better-known Lower; here on your right you will see the Woolpack Inn, built towards the close of the great wool-boom. The older inn, now Penny Hill Farm, lies about a quarter-of-a-mile from the main road, on your left, reached by a lovely little pack-pony bridge across the Esk. At Spothow nearby (the farmhouse was pulled down about 1870) a fourteenth-century ivory diptych was discovered, a beautiful example of mediæval carving: another diptych was found at not-distant Ulpha, in the Duddon valley. In mediæval times these valleys were much frequented by the Furness monks who had one of their largest sheep-farms at Brotherilkeld (termed Butterilket) in Upper Eskdale, near the old fort; indeed it is very likely that the monks used stones from the fort to build their farm. They had, at Throstle Garth, high in Upper Eskdale's head, a summer-farm or Norse-style *saeter* (*garth* is an enclosure, in Norway *guaard* is the term used for a farm-house).

The industrious monks also built a turf bank and deer-fence under Cam Spout Crag, which still makes a convenient species of causeway for those walkers who take that route to Scafell or Mickledore. However, some diversion was clearly allowed, at least for the more elevated of the brotherhood; the abbots of Furness are said to have stocked lonely and desolate Devoke Water, high on the moor above Stanley Ghyll, with red trout imported from Italy.

Eskdale's little chapel, St Catherine's, is about half-a-mile on your left from the main road, over half-a-mile indeed from central Eskdale's hamlet of Boot; delightful name. The church has a fourteenth-century window and a fourteenth-century font bowl which is said to have spent some 60 years of its long existence in a local farmhouse being used as a utensil for heaven only knows what.

In the churchyard lies Tommy Dobson, one of the most famous of all Lakeland huntsmen, Master of the Eskdale and Ennerdale fox-hounds for 53 years and now lying quietly with an interesting head-stone to his grave.

The fell-packs are followed on foot, their function not to provide fashionable sport, as in the Shires, but to catch the foxes which, in this sheep country, do much damage among lambs. One cannot really be said to advance oneself socially by following a fell pack; unless one is genuinely interested in hunting in the literal sense there is little point in indulging in it here, certainly one never meets people in the fells who say they have turned out 'just for the run', since the running here is done on Shanks' pony, over very steep rough country at an altitude often between 2,000 and 3,000 feet, more often than not in the rain and rough weather. One will seldom do less than ten miles, all in all; frequently 20 or more. Hence the reason why hunting with the fell packs has not 'caught on'; it is a purely indigenous pursuit.

Tommy Dobson, remembered as a small, rather grim-looking man, was born at Staveley in Westmorland in 1827. He was a bobbin-turner who at the age of 23 followed his trade to Eskdale.

In those days there were no large, established packs of hounds; instead each dale and hamlet had its small pack made up of hounds from individual farms and cottages. Dobson, settled in Eskdale, began hunting with his own two hounds, Cruiser and Charmer; one would like to have seen the trio out together. Tommy gradually added to his original pair of hounds and laid the foundation for a proper pack; the scattered, individually-owned local hounds one by one joined Dobson's kennels on the understanding that the local farmers and dalesmen paid him a small annual subscription, in return for which he and his pack hunted the foxes in protection of lambs and poultry. In 1883 the Eskdale and Ennerdale pack was officially formed, with Tommy as Master and Huntsman. He died in 1910, aged 83. His successor was the almost equally celebrated Willie Porter.

Beyond the Esk bridge by the schoolhouse lies Dalegarth Hall, with its wonderful old round Cumbrian chimneys, designed to beat the wind and weather whatever wind and weather might do. One of the ceilings of the house is dated 1599. Above the Hall are the falls known either as Stanley Ghyll Force (the Hall being the home of the Stanleys) or Dalegarth Force; they are the most beautiful falls in the District, but have to be walked for and moreover it is very muddy ground, generally speaking. The best view is from the overhanging cliff above the Force; this is giddy and aerial, with an impression altogether what one expects of a waterfall.

I suppose the best-known feature of Eskdale is the miniature railway, fondly known as Ratty. This fifteen-inch gauge line from Ravenglass to Boot has an interesting history.

For centuries now Eskdale granite has been mined for its iron-ore; the old mines lying in Red Ghyll on the southern side of the valley. In the early years of the last century the Whitehaven Iron Mine company commenced work at Nab Ghyll on the northern side of Eskdale, near Boot. Other mines were also opened; the South Cumberland Mine on the opposite side of the valley to Nab Ghyll and, further down the valley, the King of Prussia Inn mine. These mines were considered sufficiently productive for a narrow-gauge railway to be constructed from Ravenglass to Boot; thus was born Ratty, in 1875.

But within two years the average price of ore fell from 25 shillings a ton to 12s. 6d. a ton; as a result the Eskdale mines closed in 1876 although as the price of ore in those two years had halved so had the production of ore doubled. A frustrating state of affairs. The unfavourable state of the market also prevented the development of a good deposit of ore which had been partially opened at Brant Rake.

The mines closed; Ratty however continued to function, carrying now the red Eskdale granite and passengers. Over recent years he (one must surely call Ratty he, a sturdy, jolly little fellow) has become a firm tourist attraction; although, under the sweeping railway reforms now proposed, he is threatened. Everything about Ratty is to scale; the platforms, turn-table, level-crossings are all of moppet-size dimensions. The little engines themselves are perfect small-scale reproductions of the famous engines which cross the Rocky Mountains. All this is ridiculous, but charming. Ratty is taken very seriously by everyone; the British always take railways seriously, regarding trains as minor deities; witness the number of clergymen, bishops even, who have sought the privilege of riding on a footplate.

I remember a former Lakeland acquaintance who had a Frenchman come to stay with her; as the highlight to his visit he was driven across the District to Eskdale. In the evening the party returned. 'We have taken him for a ride on dear little Ratty!' cried the hostess, enchanted by the outing. Her guest smiled politely, but made no comment. At least the English were living up to his Gallic expectations.

Ratty is not a toy, Ratty is a serious railway, however small. To me he seems to come within the same category of oddities as General Tom Thumb, in full dress, standing on a table at Windsor in solemn audience with Queen Victoria. One must not laugh.

However, it is to be hoped that Ratty won't be closed, but survive to see his century and, indeed, much more. You should spare time, if you can, to take a ride on him.

This is all I can offer you of Eskdale if you are in a car. I could, however, walk you over the surrounding fells for days on end, for it is here, at the Woolpack to be precise, that I used to stay on family holidays when young; I was taught to walk in and about Eskdale by my father. Here, at the Woolpack, we would sometimes encounter old men whose memories of the District extended back to the days of pioneer rock-climbing and who confined themselves now to snail-slow, yet still immensely appreciative walks along the Burnmoor track, or gentle ambles from Birdhow to the foot of Cowcove Force. They were charming, in lichen-coloured tweeds, and in the evening, for a short period after dinner (for they retired to bed early), they would regale their fellow-guests with anecdotes of the Abraham Brothers when young, of when Haskett-Smith and his brother Edmund discovered the Stomach Traverse on Pillar Rock, or tales of the daring of O. G. Jones. One of these *raconteurs* was Dr Pendlebury, the very doctor himself of the Doctor's Chimney on Gable Crag; he used to tell us of how he took his dog to the Chimney, after which one had only to say 'Doctor's Chimney' to the animal and instead of dancing around excitedly anticipating a walk it would instantly hurry off on pressing other business. Dr Pendlebury, standing in the evening sunshine beneath the old sycamore that formerly sheltered the front entrance of the Woolpack, would invariably greet my sister and myself with the smiling question, 'Well, my dears, have you been up the Doctor's Chimney this afternoon?' Then, always, came the story of the dog. Dr Pendlebury was at that time well over 80.

The mountain which dominates Eskdale in its central reach is Harter Fell, one of the most beautiful in the whole District, at evening-time especially when it becomes a marvellous shade of peat-smoke, deepening to a grape-hyacinth blue. On the summit repose wonderfully weathered rocks, always reminding me of my favourite lines in my favourite poem, Wordsworth's *Resolution and Independence*, which, when he first wrote it, was entitled *The Leech Gatherer*:

> *As a huge stone is sometimes seen to lie*
> *Couched on the bald tip of some eminence;*
> *Wonder to all who do the same espy:*
> *By what means it could thither come, and whence;*
> *So that it seems a thing endued with sense:*
> *Like a sea-beast crawled forth, that on a shelf*
> *Of rock or sand reposeth, there to sun itself;*

you will find these stone sea-beasts sunning themselves, or patiently bearing the rain, throughout the District, but none are more impressive than those on Harter Fell.

Where shall we walk first? As I have said, all this is country my father taught me and although he always had much trouble getting things into my thick head, once installed they were well and truly in; thus I can conduct you round this part of the world with confidence and aplomb. What about Birker Tarn, above Birker Force; the tarn not marked on the map, but a delicious and peaty part of the world? From thence one can walk over Birker Moor to the Icelandic farmstead of Grassguards, pronounced Grassgars, one of the two most isolated habitations in the District.

All Birker Moor and Birker Fell are worth exploring; the fells above Devoke Water, the walks that take you over into Dunnerdale, skirting perhaps across the fellside above Brandy Crag to gain Birks Bridge; loveliest bridge in the District on a week-day out of the high season, but on sunny summer week-ends a favourite resort of apes (heavens, what am I saying? I mean blithe holiday-making *homo sapiens*, complete with petrol-fumes and litter). Shall we search for the Bronze Age burial cairns on Barnscar, which I mentioned in my opening chapter; well do I recall going there with my parents, they were intent and interested, while I, all seething teen-ager, wandered behind them, furious to be dragged on what I considered a tedious, time-wasting expedition looking for humps and mounds which meant nothing anyway, but holding my elders and betters in too great respect to grumble and moan outloud; my father would have given me short shrift.

By Devoke Water are narrow trods winding aimlessly through the heather, curlews, and small winds which utter thin, aching sounds. Somewhere in this vicinity, as we dropped dalewards for the lowland and civilization, I remember knocking down part of a stone wall as I climbed over it. Wordsworth, in his old age, used to knock down stone walls intentionally, smugly remarking that it was the old *sans-culotte* in him. When I knocked down this stone wall the old *sans-culotte* in my parent flashed forth with a vigour sufficient to storm the Bastille single-handed; I received a lecture on the thoughtlessness of knocking down stone walls which I have never forgotten, so that even today I have the utmost difficulty in climbing over them; I am afraid to move a limb or finger lest I dislodge a single stone. So, reader, should you similarly treat them with care amounting to reverence; they are virtually antiques, all hand-made.

The art of building them is in fact slowly dying out; people tend to replace them these days with wire-fences which are a poor substitute, offering no shelter to the sheep against foul weather (and the purpose of these walls was to shelter as well as to partition). The old wall-builders used to work summer-through, camping on the fell where their stone-walling had finished for the day and starting work with sun-rise next morning. The expert finds his stones as he goes along; the walls are usually built some four feet six inches high, say two feet six inches wide at the base, narrowing as they ascend. They are secured by large stones called 'throughs'; because they are large enough to extend completely through the wall. A good wall should be almost a foot narrower at the top than at the bottom; the centre of the lower half of the wall is filled in with rubble. No cement or fixative is used; the stones lock one another. Hence the name dry stone-walling. Sloping cam stones (*cam*, a crest, a cock's comb) are placed on top. In some walls you will find that 'throughs' have been placed ladder-wise so that you can get over the wall; you should look out for these. In the base of the wall you will see, at intervals, square holes; these are hogg-holes, provided for the hoggs (sheep) to pass through.

Shall we, while we are in Eskdale, do the so-called Postman's Terrace-Walk? This is picked up at Gill Bank half-a-mile above Boot, up Whillan Beck, most delectable for its junipers and wonderful scents. Here there once lived a species of hermit who made wooden bowls and curiosities from ash wood, soaking them in the beck to enhance their graining and colour. The old pack-pony way goes from here across Burn Moor to Wasdale, but we turn right from Gill Bank to follow a trod, rather than a track, first to Eel Tarn, then to Stony Tarn, and from thence traversing along the contour of the fellside to keep well above the ground falling away from us into the valley. We go by Peel Place Noddle (or Naddle) to cross Cowcove Beck as it is called on the map, though it is more generally known as Scale Beck. Here we abandon the postman's old route (a postman who delivered his letters on foot) to make our way on to Slight Side; in reality a very large, bulging side, the backside of Scafell in fact. He, the king of the giants, looks, when approached from this angle, very different from his magnificent, northern-faced self; here he is bland, tawny-green, rolling upwards in great slabs of muscular flesh, as it were, like one of Rubens's massive figures. It is worth remembering, when you fell-walk, that each mountain has a grandly sculptured, precipitous northern face and a comparatively mild, smoothly bulging backside, turf or heather covered; if you lose your bearings do not attempt to descend the dangerous northern face but walk directly away from it until you discover the southern, safer rear; down this you can go without much difficulty. You may end up in the wrong valley, but at least you are off the mountain which we will suppose you wished to be because there was mist, or a blizzard, or night was quickly falling. Never, however, try to follow a beck downwards; it may seem a good safe way of getting off a mountain but in fact it is dangerous, for becks have steep, often hidden waterfalls and where the water suddenly tumbles over a rocky pitch you may well tumble too. People have lost their lives in this way.

If you don't wish to leave the Postman's Terrace for Slight Side you may continue along the terrace contour by High Scarth Crag and so to Cam Spout. Clearly no postman came delivering letters here; there is nobody to expect the post. From Cam Spout ascend good, so-called quick routes on to Scafell and Mickledore, as I think I have already said. On no account try Cam Spout on a hot day, unless you wish to know what it is to be a spider crawling up the inside of a dry, sun-baked drain-pipe.

Yours is all Upper Eskdale to explore, barren, beautiful, deserted, littered with the debris of glaciers. Bowfell, Esk Pike, Ewer Gap await you; in Throstle Garth are remains of stone walls which are all that is left now as evidence of the Furness flockmasters. Upper Eskdale is strenuous going, but it is heaven for a strong and agile walker who is fonder of exploring a small area and getting to know it intimately rather than of merely clocking up an impressive mileage. A 12-mile day here is worth a 30-mile trek on the flat.

You can, of course, gain Slight Side from Hardrigg Beck above Burnmoor Tarn, swinging right a little on to Broad Tongue, or by crossing the little bridge for Great How, before you reach the tarn. Burn Moor is named not for burns, in the Scots meaning, but for the *borrans*, or heaps of stones found upon the moor, these Burn Moor borrans being small Bronze Age cairns and stone-circles.

This Burn Moor track is the old corpse-road from Wasdale Head to Eskdale Green, for in the old days there was no burial-ground at Wasdale. It is the route you will take, from Eskdale, if you are on a walking-tour of the District; after your stay in Eskdale, either probably at the Woolpack or the Burnmoor Inn at Boot (for below Boot is too low down the valley for a walker) you will shoulder your rucksack and take this track across the lonely moor, past the large, melancholy tarn.

Motorists, although deprived of the solitudes of Burn Moor, can make up for it by exploring Ravenglass (a walker can, of course, take a day off from walking to visit Ravenglass on Ratty, but one becomes loath to spare even a day from Upper Eskdale). The old Roman port is now land-locked and has a deserted atmosphere which is attractive in this overcrowded age. The Roman bath-house, already mentioned, was apparently used, after the Romans had left, by the Penningtons who were lords of the Ravenglass manor. Sometime in the late twelfth century they moved into a pele-tower and this, in 1325, was enlarged into a castle. The present Muncaster Castle was built on the same site in 1800. Henry VI stayed at the old castle in 1461; as a gift of thanks to Sir John Pennington for his hospitality the King presented a greenish-glass bowl, the so-called 'Luck of Muncaster' for, 'whyllys the family shold kepe hit unbrecken, they shold gretely thrif' and never lack a male heir. This bowl (still unbroken) is even now at the castle, together with the bedstead the King is said to have slept on, and a portrait of him holding the 'Luck'.

Existent too is a portrait of Tom Skelton, Tom Fool of Muncaster, in service to the Penningtons in the first half of the seventeenth century.

Professional fools, whether in historical anecdote or as portrayed in Shakespearian drama, seem singularly tedious; whether they were mentally sick, or simply rascals on to what seemed an easy way of earning a living it is difficult to decide. Their wit was of the riddle-me-ree sort, much esteemed in former times, while their pranks were often horribly cruel. Tom Skelton seems to have had a particularly sadistic streak in him. Were Fools psychotics?

Tom, most truculent-looking, displays his Will, written in doggerel and clearly intended as a witty composition, but the key to the wit has now been lost and all falls flat.

Also at Muncaster Castle are the various Roman findings from Hard Knott. The grounds only are open to the public.

For Wastwater you take the road from Eskdale Green to Gosforth and from thence you turn north for Strands. At Gosforth is the famous Viking Cross I mentioned in the opening chapter of this book. You are now within true Icelandic territory.

CHAPTER SEVEN

Wasdale Head

As you drive northwards alongside Wastwater, on the road from Strands, you see at the head of the lake Gavel Neese. A gavel is the old name for a gable and from this angle the Gable mountain is most aptly named; a high Tudor gable from which the Neese or *ness* (nose) runs down, it appears from here, to the lake margin. In point of fact Gable is some two miles from the head of Wastwater. It is a wonderful view, this long look up Wastwater to Gavel Neese, one of the two best in the District, the other being the magnificent sight of Great Gable from the north when he presents the aspect of the huge, domed head of an Icelandic god. You won't obtain this northern view of him from any road; one of the north-western fells must be scaled if you wish to see Gable thus. Moreover you must avoid a warm day, for then his features will flatten into haze and his wonderful face, scarred by precipices and topped by massive brow, will be, as it were, averted from you. You must try to catch him, in summer, on a fine morning before eight, on a fine evening after seven or so, or on any cool cloudy day when the sky is high and windy enough for the cloud to be raised above him. Majesty always stipulates the times when audience may be granted.

The journey up Wastwater is noteworthy for the famous Screes, cascading in stone-shoots from crag high above. However, they are far more beautiful in winter than in summer; indeed Wastwater and Wasdale are at their best, for sheer colour variations alone, in autumn, winter or early spring. The appearance of these central fells is then marvellously subtle and complex. Snow on the tops and in the gullies emphasises their inherent savagery.

Wasdale Head is a cul-de-sac of dark fells crowding round a glacially carved basin of intake-fields patterned by stone walls, a small hamlet with a famous hotel, an old pack-pony bridge, a tiny chapel, a well-known farm and two passes, neither possible for motors; the Sty climbing up between Gable and Lingmell, leading you either over into Borrowdale or on to Esk Hause, the District's main highway, while the track winding up Mosedale leads to the Black Sail pass and Ennerdale. There is nothing for you to do at Wasdale Head except walk or climb; the definition of walking being that you proceed without using your hands. When you start using your hands it becomes scrambling. Climbing means you require a rope. When people say they have climbed Great Gable they mean they have been for a walk up Great Gable, perhaps with a little scrambling thrown in. When and if you climb you do it *on* Great Gable, or whichever mountain your climbs are found upon.

Wasdale Head is an ancient Icelandic settlement. Although it was the Danes who sacked and harried north-east England, to settle in Yorkshire and Lincolnshire, it was the Norse who came to Cumberland and Westmorland. The origin of the Norse is deeply obscure. Iceland was the country from which they embarked to engage upon their astonishingly adventurous voyaging and colonising, but they had first conquered and colonised Iceland, arriving there from some other shore; which shore nobody has yet decided with any certainty. From Iceland they swept south, colonising the Faroes, Shetlands, Orkneys, the west coast of Scotland, Ireland, the Isle of Man. We know that some of them reached Newfoundland. It was from the Isle of Man that exploring crews sailed to the coast of Cumberland, supposedly landing at a point between St Bees Head and Humphrey Head. The Norsemen found Cumberland to their taste; highly reminiscent of Iceland itself, but the climate not so cold. From invaders they developed into settlers, building up a number of small, isolated communities which have more or less persisted down to the present day.

These Norse were the forebears of the Cumbrian statesmen; a statesman being one who owned and gained his whole livelihood from a little farm with which went a small acreage of garth and intake-fields. With the farm also went a flock of sheep, the flock being apportioned a certain share of fellside, the *heaf*. Each farm had its own recognised drift-

118

road (*edrift road*, a road for driving sheep) across the land between the points where the farm property stopped and the heaf began.

The old-style statesmen have now virtually vanished, although the tradition is still maintained of the flock being let or sold with the property. The Icelandic small-holdings or estates have developed into larger farms; economic conditions have changed.

The Norse settlers built habitations of wattle-and-daub and wood, around which were stone-wall enclosed intake-fields. Further stone-walls were built on the fells to mark the heafs and also to provide protection for sheep against foul weather. Icelandic became the language of the country; it is still the basis of the old Cumberland dialect (it was De Quincey who first investigated the possibility that the Lake District dialect and place-names were of largely Viking origin).

It is also believed that the Norsemen introduced the Herdwick sheep; a breed peculiar to this District.

Sheep; they are everywhere up here. As I write now a small flock of them is pattering through the yard beneath my window, the air is thick with their bleating, the barking of sheep-dogs, the imprecations of the shepherd who is having trouble with one particularly foolish ewe and her lamb. On the opposite side of this narrow valley two more shepherds and their dogs are driving a flock across a circular intake-field, towards a gate to the drift-road which leads to their farm. High on the fell-side, well above the drift-road, amongst rocks and long neglected slagheaps of an ancient disused mine wander more sheep which have not yet been gathered; they bleat in sympathy with the flock below. All the bleating has a compulsive note. It is clipping-time; early July, time for the thick woollen coats to be sheared. Day after day the shepherds go out with their dogs, sheep-gathering on the fells, returning with flocks which are placed in the intake-fields close to the farms. Later, when the clipping is over, the sheep will be returned to the fell.

Sheep here are an integral part of the scenery; one might well regard them as a topographical feature. Therefore you should know at least a little about them. Before I go further may I ask you not on any account to feed sheep if they approach you and your car. Farmers are adamant about this; the sheep get into the habit of wandering by the road, looking for motorists to feed them and the roadway spells injury for

17 *Looking up Wastwater to Great Gable*

them. When a sheep comes to the roadside, hopefully looking at you for something to eat (the animal isn't hungry, merely gutsy) give a loud shoo and drive it off. You are doing both sheep and farmer a service.

There are some 33 separate breeds of sheep in the British Isles; they are divided into two main groups, mountain and lowland. The Herdwick sheep is the hardiest of all British breeds, with the coarsest wool, which is not of very high value on the market. Your pure-bred Herdwick is white-faced, the ewes are hornless, both sexes are, comparatively speaking, small in size. Pure-bred Herdwicks have unfortunately become increasingly rare since more and more farmers have taken to Herdwicks crossed with Swaledale, or Herdwicks crossed with Blackface. Herdwick wool fetches less than Swaledale, on the other hand a Herdwick will have more wool on it. I have been told, however, that a renewed interest in the pure Herdwick breed is growing and you will find Lakeland farms where great pride is taken in a flock of pure-bred Herdwicks.

Herdwick mutton used to be considered a great Lakeland delicacy; the flavour is delicious, but it is somewhat too fat for the modern taste. There is, somewhat unexpectedly, a small but discerning market for it in Manchester.

The females are called gimmers, the males are wethers, or wedders. During their first winter, however, they are all hoggs, or hoggets, irrespective of their sex. They remain hoggs until the ensuing spring, when they become shearlings; a gimmer shearling, a wedder shearling. After a second winter they become twinters and thereafter they graduate to becoming staid ewes and tups.

The first year in a sheep's life is spent, after birth in spring, by summer on the fells, the young lamb with its mother. From November to April of this first year the lambs (now termed hoggs) are wintered in the lowlands. With their second spring the hoggs become shearlings and return to the fells with the ewes. Autumn and their second winter sees them graduated into twinters, now the gimmers are put to the ram. After they have had their first lamb they become ewes. Rams are known as tups unless castrated, when they remain wedders.

The habit of mountain sheep is to sleep at night on the tops, descending the mountain slopes at dawn, then slowly to graze their way upwards until by evening they have regained the tops. It is one of the duties of a shepherd to see that the lower grazing levels are not eaten off in the good weather; these valley-bottom grazing grounds must be kept for winter. It was from this routine of high-level summer grazing that the Norsemen developed their *saeters* or summer-farms; these former *saeters* are still occupied and farmed, but now all the year round. The old name is still traced in such contemporary names as Seatoller, Seathwaite. It is wonderful to think of the centuries of unbroken history which lie behind these Lakeland sheep-farms; Skelghyll in Newlands, for instance, has been in the hands of one family and always a sheep-farm since 1347 for a certainty and in all likelihood since much earlier than that.

The sheep have constantly to be gathered from the fells for those ceremonies which mark the shepherd's year. The first sheep-gathering comes when the ewes are brought in for dipping and feeding before lambing. In summer ewes and lambs are fetched again from the fell for clipping, later for dipping to cleanse the wool. And in autumn come the big sheep-gatherings when ewes and hoggets are once again brought down from the fells and the fortunate hoggets are sent off to their winter grazing grounds.

Sheep are subject to a wide variety of diseases. In summer they are in danger from the blow-fly which frequents the bracken. One blow-fly can lay so many eggs in a sheep's fleece that within 24 hours the wool will have become a writhing mass of maggots intent upon devouring the living sheep. Besides being troubled by maggots, or 'wicks' as they are called, the animals are beset by tapeworms, which cause 'sturdies' or brain-cysts. Tick diseases are rife, or would be without regular dipping. Liver-fluke is contracted by parasites from muddy ground. Animals which graze in areas where the soil is deficient in cobalt and copper-sulphate become what is termed 'souted'; they lose weight and sicken. Carrion-crows pick out the eyes of weak lambs, or of sick and dying ewes. Weasels will attack lambs lying weak and helpless. Foxes worry the ewes and kill the lambs, tearing out their entrails, particularly relishing lambs' liver.

Fell-sheep are astonishingly agile, yet will occasionally become crag-bound, grazing further and further out upon a narrow ledge across a precipice face until the animal can go no further. There is no way up, no way down, no room for the sheep to turn round on the ledge. If not discovered and rescued the creature will die of starvation.

A fell-sheep buried in winter snow can survive for as long, some-times, as a fortnight; each sheep in a little snow-cavern of its own can breathe through a snowdrift where a man would die for lack of oxygen. The sheep keeps very warm in his snow-chamber, like an eskimo in an igloo, but if rain falls and is then followed by frost, forming an ice-plate over the snow, oxygen is thereby excluded. It is in such weather-conditions that shepherds become anxious and start digging out their sheep. It is said that the dogs which are stupidest at driving sheep often make the best 'markers' when it comes to finding sheep buried in snow.

The Border Collie is the world's most famous breed of sheep-dog; a breed at least 350 years old and said to have originated in Scotland. The best modern strain comes from a Northumberland stock 60 years old. The dogs are commanded by signals and whistles and readers who have not attended a sheep-dog trial should make every effort to do so. These take place each year in Lakeland, during summer, at Apple-thwaite, Windermere, Rydal and Threlkeld. One may also be lucky enough to see a shepherd and his dogs actually at work rounding sheep on a fell. 'Gang ahint!' is the traditional command to a dog to fall into the rear of the sheep and to collect lagging or straying members of the flock.

One could write a great deal about sheep-dogs; I have several of them as my neighbours. They are essentially working dogs; I am not very much in favour of people who try to keep them merely as domestic companions. The Border Collie is a low-slung animal that should be lean, with a sleek coat. His eyes are attentive and tawny, he will stand looking at you courteously but with reserve, mouth slightly open, pink tongue curling out between brilliantly white teeth. A Border Collie can stalk sheep running crouched on his belly like a fox, flattening him-self to the ground and becoming virtually invisible. The speed, skill and sagacity of these dogs is wonderful and they work with their masters in a manner which has convinced me, after much close observa-tion, that a certain degree of telepathy is involved.

What breed of sheep-dog the Norsemen used we do not know; we must suppose that they used them, a dog is an integral part of a shepherd. The presumed Icelandic system of counting sheep certainly survived down to this century, although it has now ceased to be used; the last old men who counted their sheep,

'Yan, tan, tether, mether, pimp,
Teezar, leezar, catterah, horna, dick,
Yan-dick, tan-dick, tether-dick, mether-dick, bumpit,
Yan-a-bumpit, tan-a-bumpit, tedera-bumpit, medera-bumpit,
   gigot . . .'

having been gathered to their forefathers. This fascinating rigmarole is now handed down as a curiosity; I myself was taught it by a charming young man in Borrowdale some 20 years ago. But I should much like to know how the gigot got into it, a *gigot* being, as every good gourmet knows, a leg of mutton (preferably cooked *à la Gasconnade*).

It will be seen that these delightful numerals only go up to 20. The twenties were counted on the fingers of each hand and if the flock were large enough to exhaust the supply of fingers (ten twenties) one went on to marking off the twenties with pebbles. One can imagine some horribly confused Icelandic shepherds standing checking their sheep one by one through a gap; sheep, dogs, fingers and pebbles being a lot to contend with at once.

The ancient system of marking sheep for identity is still used. The bible of every flockmaster is *Gate's Shepherd's Guide for Cumberland, Westmorland and Lancashire*, the classic of smit books (a book of sheep markings). Before me as I write lies the 1879 edition, very kindly lent to me by my neighbour; it seems to be the first edition, with a photograph of the bewhiskered Mr Gate himself on the title-page and a brief introduction expressing the hope that the guide will prove of benefit and assistance to all flockmasters. Turning the leaves of this book one sees, on page after page after page, two identical sheep, a ram and a ewe, bucolic and very woolly, standing facing one another, smiling sweetly, on the same strip of grass under the same tree. But see, in every sketch the smits, or markings which the sheep bear, are different; also in each sketch the animals wear fresh pairs of ears, always notched or slit in a different pattern. Every flockmaster in the District, or almost every flockmaster (a few seem to have failed to subscribe) has his sheep portrayed; the sketches are colourless save for the red or blue smits. Under the sketches we read at random,

'Moses DOVER: High Snab, Newlands: under-halved near, forked far, pop on near side.

William HODGSON: Aiken: under-halved both, blue pop on top of shoulders.

Edward NELSON: Gatesgarth, Buttermere: Fleetwith Stock, under key-bitted near, two strokes over couplings, wethers black on head, twinters red.

John CANNON: Watendlath: High Fell Stock, cropped far, upper fold bitted near. Gimmer sheep, black pop on top of shoulders, Wethers, stroke over couplings, Twinters, red behind head.

Towers TYSON: Paddockwray: cropped near, under-halved far, pop on back of head, and one on tail head.'

The smit marks are either in the form of strokes or pops, a pop being a round blob of colour, the colours used for marking being either red or blue. The ear notchings and slittings are more complicated; under-halved means that half the ear has been notched out on the under side, forked means a forked-shaped notching, key-bitted is a square notch. A ritted ear is one that has been slit down the centre; sometimes one sees a double-ritted, or double slitted ear. Each ear, of course, has a top and bottom side. With strokes and pops on various parts of the body, notchings, croppings and slittings of the top-sides or bottom-sides of near or far side ears, not to mention horn burns which are also used, the supply of possible variations in sheep marking seems inexhaustible. The expert can tell by one glance which flock a sheep belongs to.

Mrs Heelis (Beatrix Potter) was a keen breeder of Herdwicks and in one of the show-cases of original manuscripts at Hill Top Farm you will see a small note-book containing a water-colour sketch on one page and scrawled, on the opposing page, notes of High Snab and Birkrigg sheep markings.

Mr Gate, in his 1876 edition, hit on the admirable notion of inviting leading local flockmasters to contribute essays on Herdwick sheep. William Abbott of Coniston in his essay claimed that the ideal Herdwick should have 'a strong, flowing coat, standing up around the neck, resembling, as it were, a lion'. There should be no specks upon the face or legs; such specks did not belong to a pure-bred Herdwick. 'This beautiful and useful animal can stand the rain and hail, can brave the strongest blasts which sweep these northern hills . . . and I know from experience that the intensity of the storms is terrible, blowing, as it frequently does upon these fells, a perfect hurricane . . .'. The author then continues: 'What is there so charming anywhere in the resources of animated nature as a lovely Herdwick—beautiful to look upon, and useful . . .? Who would not feel just a little proud to see them rolling down the mountain breasts at times of washing and shearing, going mostly on land where nothing else could live upon, with fleeces flowing, and through their noses blowing?

> *May the flocks on the mountains still thrive and increase,*
> *May their owners still live in contentment and peace!*
> *May health attend each, as through life they do go,*
> *Is the wish of the writer, whose name's found below*
>
> William Abbott, *Coniston.*'

One feels that this author had come under the influence of his neighbour, Ruskin. The next essay is very different in style and flavour, written by Edward Nelson from the famous Gatesgarth sheep-farm in Buttermere and John Wilson of Keskadale, Newlands:

'. . . we give it as our firm opinion that a good coat is the first and most important point in judging a Herdwick. . . . The ears should be white and sharp, and stand well up, as any tendency to droop betokens a want of spirit to grapple with hill life. In colour the head should be light grey, with a hoar-frost nose, a rustiness about the poll, as well as a lion-like mane. These are all solid requirements. The body should be shaped like a barrel, the legs well to the outside; a broad breast, placed forward as the forequarters are chiefly relied on both for constitution and the scales. The knees should be strong, and the bone thin to fetlock; and then a big white foot to follow. The hind-legs to spring from a well-muttoned thigh, thin shaped, with plenty of bristles, looking rather upwards. The tail to reach no further down than the camerals, and thick at the root. A sheep should be well ribbed up, the greater their power to endure hunger; the back broad, and well filled in behind the shoulders; when turned up to have a deep and broad breast, with soft, kindly wool upon it. . . .'

It was Coleridge who remarked upon the high calibre of 'the thoughts, feelings, language and manners of the shepherd-farmers in

the vales of Cumberland and Westmorland'.[1] This he attributed partly
to their independence and partly to the fact that what education they
received was of a very high order. Their style of thought and speech
also benefited, thought Coleridge, from much reading of the Bible and
liturgy. '. . . the mountaineers, whose manners have been so often
eulogized, are in general better educated and greater readers than men
of equal rank elsewhere . . .'[1]

Wasdale Head is a typical Cumbrian sheep-farming hamlet that
could not have changed much from Icelandic times until 1840 or so
when tourists first started to penetrate these inner dales and a centuries-
old way of life inevitably began to change under outside influences.

There lived at Wasdale Head a statesman, Will Ritson, one of Lakeland's most celebrated personalities; yet there have been many others
like him, there still are many like him, he gained celebrity because he
was a great personal friend of the well-known Professor Wilson of
Elleray, Windermere, and because, almost accidentally, he made
Wasdale Head a rock-climbing centre.

Ritson, born at Row Foot, Wasdale Head, in 1808, grew up to be a
keen fox-hunter and wrestler. At an early age he became huntsman to
Mr Rawson of Wasdale Hall, then to Mr Huddleston of Gosforth.
Later Ritson was able to form and maintain a pack of his own. His love
of local sports brought him into contact with Wilson, a giant of a man,
fanatically devoted to fell-running, wrestling, sailing (he was nicknamed *The Lord High Admiral of Windermere*), cock-fighting and fox-
hunting. Heir to a large fortune, he fell in love with Windermere as a
very young man, bought a cottage there, at Elleray, and later built a
house there. He became a professor of Moral Philosophy at Edinburgh
and earned literary distinction as *Christopher North* on the editorial staff
of *Blackwood's*. He was one of Sir Walter Scott's greatest friends. Wilson
enjoyed the distinction of belonging not only to the Lakeland circle of
Wordsworth, Professor Sedgwick, De Quincey and the rest, but his
love of sport brought him, as I have said, into contact with Ritson and
Ritson introduced Wilson to his own Lakeland sporting circles.
Besides being a great sportsman Wilson possessed tremendously high
spirits and sense of fun. Ritson, for his part, was a great wit and racon-
teur in true Cumbrian style and there is no doubt that the two men

[1] *Biographia Literaria*, chap. xvii, 1817.

18   *Great Gable: south face*

provided one another with the kind of company each most enjoyed. Wilson introduced Ritson to his literary friends; they found Ritson delightful. Ritson, courteously, expressed himself equally charmed by the company of Wordsworth, Professor Sedgwick and the rest. It was, however, Wilson who provided real liaison between the two groups; apparently equally at home with either.

The literary and academic gentlemen flocked increasingly to Wasdale Head for talk and a crack with Ritson; by 1856 Ritson was receiving so many visitors at his little farmhouse he decided to exploit the situation, obtained a licence and renamed his ancient home the Huntsman Inn. Hospitality was simple, but the host's personality ensured success. We are told, for instance, the following tale:

One night at the inn discussion arose on the subject of marriage and one visitor, a young man, perhaps trying to impress the company with his worldly wisdom, aired the opinion that a man should always marry for money. Ritson said:

'That's t' verra warst thing thoo cud think o' deein'. Auld Dinah theer' (his wife) 'had a five pound nwoate, an' Aa nivver 'eeard t' last on 't.'

Auld Dinah, it should be observed, also came from ancient local lineage, having been before her marriage a Fletcher of Nether Wasdale. In her own quiet way she possessed a personality as powerful as that of her husband.

With Ritson's help Wilson organised an annual wrestling contest at the Ferry Inn, Windermere, which became an increasingly important sporting event to which fell-racing, hound-trailing and so forth were added. In 1861 these sports moved to Grasmere; thus originated the biggest annual sports-meeting of the North. It might be noted here that the heavyweight championship of the Westmorland and Cumberland wrestling carries with it the title of World Champion.

De Quincey has left us pleasant glimpses[1] of Professor Wilson in Ambleside society; here is the Professor at a *soirée dansante*, given at the house of Charles Loyd where, says De Quincey, 'I first saw Professor Wilson, in circumstances of animation, and buoyant with youthful spirits, under the excitement of lights, wine, and above all, female company. He, by the way, was the best male dancer (not professional)

[1] *Recollections of the Lakeland Poets.*

131

I have ever seen; and this advantage he owed entirely to the extra-ordinary strength of his foot in all parts, to its peculiarly happy con-formation, and to the accuracy of his ear; for, as to instruction, I have often understood from his family he never had any. . . .'

Wilson (a very happily married man) was immensely popular with the ladies; could they but have seen him enjoying himself in that other and very different Lakeland society he frequented they might not have smiled quite so sweetly upon him. Here is Ritson describing Wilson at another evening's entertainment:

'Aa remember, theer was a murry neet[1] at Wasd'le Head that verra time, an' Wilson an' t'aad Parson was theer amang t' rest. When they'd gitten a bit on, Wilson mead a sang aboot t' parson. He mead it reet off t' stick end. He began wi t' parson fust, then he got to t' Pope, an' then he turn'd it to th' divil, an' sic like, till he hed 'em fallin' off theer cheers wi' fun. Parson was quite stunn'd, an' rayder vex't an a', but at last he burst oot laughin' wi' t' rest.'

Mountains, as we have seen, were important to the Romantic Movement. Mountaineering as a sport was virtually unknown until the later years of the eighteenth century when, in 1786, Mont Blanc was first climbed by Dr Paccard and a chamois hunter named Jacques Balmat, largely because the great scientist, De Saussure, had offered a reward to anyone who should scale it. He himself climbed the moun-tain the following year, an Englishman followed suit a week later. As a result the Alps were gradually opened up and mountaineering became a popular sport, although patronised almost entirely in the first years by scientists and intellectuals; indeed it always has been and even today still tends to be a sport with an intellectual appeal. It was the English, chiefly, who developed the Alps as a climbing ground, conquering the major peaks and in fact being responsible for the growth of the sport in general. In England intellect is more often than not accompanied by strong leg muscles and an almost monk-like desire to subject the body to gruelling endurance-tests; the English reaction to a person who chooses to spend his holiday relaxing in a deck-chair is to suspect the quality of his grey-matter. At all events the English opened up climbing both in the Alps and upon British hills. It might fairly be said that the

[1] A shepherds' murry neet (merry night): an ancient Lakeland revelry which we shall be dealing with in a later chapter.

first real explorer of the Lake District mountains was Coleridge, who had an endearing habit of walking by moonlight from Keswick to Grasmere taking in Helvellyn on the way; he was also the first known person to climb Broad Stand, the tricky little rock-face which bars Scafell from the Pike by direct route. Wordsworth, too, was one of the leading pioneers of British mountains. It was true that shepherds and fox-hunters had travelled over the fells for many years, leaving the marked tracks to go where their sheep or their hunting took them, but in Britain it was the poets who first climbed purely for the sake of the mountains.

Professor J. D. Forbes went to the Alps as a scientist and developed into a leading mountaineer. Professor Tyndall went to the Alps to examine the structure of glaciers and also became an addict of mountaineering. Other names must include Alfred Wills, the Rev. Charles Hudson, Charles Carrington, E. S. Kennedy, Frederick Morshead and Leslie Stephen.

In 1857 the Alpine Club was formed. In 1856, as we have seen, Ritson had opened his inn; among his patrons were many Alpine Club members.

Some of the less experienced visitors demanded the services of a local guide and often Ritson would oblige them himself, leading them tranquilly up Scafell, the Pikes, Great Gable, Pillar; for these were places over which he had hunted and gathered sheep all his life. No doubt he frequently wondered what all the mountaineering fuss was about. Some of the people who came to admire the mountains were not at all to his liking and there is an account of one occasion when a particularly annoying Bishop was taken to the summit of the Scafell Pikes and deposited by the final cairn with the Ritson observation: 'Well, here y'are, Mister Bishop; as near Heaven as ye'll ever be.'

Climbing to the summits of the mountains began to be followed by rock-climbing proper; the enthusiasts devoting themselves not to ascending to the tops but simply to scaling the crags. This thoroughly puzzled Ritson, who sardonically asked the rock-climbers if the fells weren't high enough for them? But the best Ritson remark is the one he once made to a visitor who came from London and was unwise enough to say, 'Fancy living here all your life! Why don't you come to London, Mr Ritson, and see some of the sights?'

'Ah, m'lad', replied Ritson, 'theer's nea 'cashion for us t' cum up t' Lunnon t' see t' seets, 'cos sum o' t' seets cums doon here t' see us.'

The Ritsons retired from running the inn in 1879 and the Tysons took over. The present hotel was built a few years later, the original inn remaining as an annexe. The celebrated Whitings, relatives of the Ritsons, ran the hotel until recently; Mr and Mrs Wilson Pharoah now have it.

The hotel became one of the most famous climbing hostelries in the world; many are the tales told of the *Wastwater Hotel*, of which more will be said in the next chapter. Ritson himself died at Strands in 1890, at the age of 83, talking almost to the very last, it is said, of the local hunt. To commemorate him Baddeley named a small waterfall not far from the hotel 'Ritson Force' and as such it now appears on the map.

The Ritson style of wit, very dry and to the point, flourishes in Cumberland. Many of his neighbours matched him with their comments; Ritson himself was particularly fond of telling the story of a farmer in Nether Wasdale who, with a farm-lad, had built a tall hay-stack. The stack finished, the boy shouted down from the top of it where he was perched, 'Meeaster, hoo is Aa to git doon?' The farmer shouted back, 'Shut thee 'ees an' walk aboot a bit.'

Some of the humour is of a leg-pulling kind, always done with a dead-pan expression, accompanied by a courteous manner. Not long ago I heard the following conversation on the local bus, between a lady visitor and the conductor.

'Please, can you tell me, is there a Marks and Spencer's in Keswick?'

'Aye, and a good branch of Selfridge's too.'

The following is a local shaggy-dog story,[1] of somewhat more contemporary vintage than the Ritson tales:

One evening, when some farmers were sitting in their local inn, their dogs at their feet, the door opened and a stranger entered, accompanied by a very large, yellow dog. The stranger went to the bar and ordered a drink, the dog seating itself on its haunches beside him. The farmers, though unwilling to appear rude, couldn't take their eyes off the yellow dog and at last one of them said, 'Excuse me for asking, meeaster, but what manner o' dog is yon?'

[1] I am indebted to Peter Hosking for repeating this story to me. The original source is shrouded in some mystery.

'I couldna rightly name t' breed,' replied the stranger, 'he was a present to th' wife, but I'll tell ye wan thing, he's a richt gay fichter, is yon dog.'
'Oh ay?'
'Aye.'
'I've me own dog here', said the farmer, after a pause. 'He's a gay bonny fichter too, is yon.'
'Oh ay?'
'Aye.'
Another pause. Then says the farmer, 'Tell ye what, are ye willing to match yon dog o' yourn agin mine?'
'Aye.'
So the dogs were matched, the yellow dog against the farmer's dog, and the onlookers gathered round, expecting a good fight, but the dogs had scarcely gone into action when snip snap! went the yellow dog's jaws and poor Lay-Doon lay dead.
There was a longish silence, then one of the farmers said, 'Ye're reet, meeaster, yon dog's a gay bonny fichter, but I've a dog can beat yon.'
'Oh ay?'
'Aye.' Another pause, then the farmer says, 'Are ye game to match my dog agin yon?'
'Aye.'
So the second dog was stirred forth from under the chair where he lay and was matched against the yellow dog. But once again, no sooner had the dogs started to fight than snip snap! went the yellow dog's jaws and poor Lay-Doon lay dead.
'Aa-ah, ye're reet', said a third farmer, 'yon's a rare bonny fichter hooiver; but I've a dog oop at farm will beat yon.'
'Oh ay?'
'Aye.' Another pause, then, 'Shall I gang anant an' fetch him?'
'Aye.'
So the farmer went back home and returned with his dog and the onlookers once more gathered round and the two dogs were set to fight. But once more, before seconds had elapsed, snip snap! went the yellow dog's jaws and poor Lay-Doon lay dead.
'Ah, ye're reet, ye're reet', said the landlord of the inn, 'I niver

set ees on a bonnier fichter than yon blake beast o' yourn. What breed o' dog did ye say he was ?'

'I didna', said the stranger, 'to tell t' truth I dooan't reetly know t' breed o' yon dog. My son fetched him home from Africa as a present for t' wife, like. Aye, an' a fremmed-lookin' beast he was, till we fetched t' shears an' clipped off a gurt kind o' mane he had growin' a' aboot t' shoulders.'

And now, reader, I will leave you to rest, while I try to borrow a pair of boots for you; tomorrow we shall be going up Scafell together.

CHAPTER EIGHT

Central Massif

The morning, when we start, has a thick drizzle in it and as we climb up the Sty under Gable the cloud presses down on the Napes to our left, only a few hundred feet above us. The air smells of rain and wet stone, with a touch of sheep. We can hear no sound but the trudge of our feet up the track and Lingmell Beck foaming in the bottom. Lingmell itself, a low-thrusting, buttress-like limb of the Scafell Pikes, lies in a dark grey and purple wall across the beck, but we cannot see how high the mountains are here or what they are like because of the low cloud, which cuts all from view above the 2,000 foot contour or thereabouts.

Below and behind us lie the intricately-patterned intake-fields of Wasdale Head, with Burnthwaite Farm as the last place of habitation in the dale. We proceed up the Sty, most famous of passes; a narrow, twisting, steep route over and between boulders (a *sty* is a pass). The old pack-pony route runs on the other side of Lingmell Beck, descending from the Furness-built causeway, still discernible near the head of the pass, then proceeding by the beck-bottom. The path we are on was a quicker, contour-hugging track, an old shepherds' trod: when the pack-trains ceased the old route fell into disuse and this shepherds' track became the accepted way up this side of the Sty.

We continue to slog upwards; the rain comes down more heavily, making a lively, albeit rather savage sound on the rocks around us. The air is full of water and you murmur that we shall get soaked. I reply yes, we shall get soaked, but once soaked we have nothing more to worry about. To divert your attention from the soaking, part and parcel of walking upon British hills, I point out that we are now passing, on our left, a great expanse of rock-face that is the famous climbing-ground of Kern Knotts, at which we will look more closely presently, while across the narrow valley on our right, rending the fell-side, is an immeasurably gloomy slit-trench of a ghyll; over and before it moves a fragmented curtain of cloud so that a distinct view of the ghyll is impossible, all is rain and dark cavities, but the overall impression is excessively forbidding. This is Piers Ghyll and somewhere in its recesses runs the young Lingmell Beck, its source high above, between the Pike and Broad Crag. You will know more about it in a little while.

We are almost at the head of the Sty, now; a faint wind greets us and the cloud, now all about us, rolls and surges, while the track dodges about between even larger boulders. You know now the answer to those persons who ask if a car cannot be got over the Sty? From this point, looking back, one has a marvellous view of Wastwater; no longer a glittering pale blue lake but a sinister loch, gleaming with shades of pewter and plum. The glaciers seem to have departed from this scene only yesterday.

And now we have reached the famous Sty Head; the District's Piccadilly Circus as I gaily inform you. You look around. Not a soul in sight. Rain and cloud bowl together over a small expanse of tummocky, marshy ground where the only sign of civilisation is a spider's-web of faint tracks, meeting at a point by a large boulder and a battered finger-post. On the lee-side of this is a place to sit and a First-Aid chest: in this cheery spot we sit down to eat a piece of Kendal Mint while I unfold the map to show you where we are. Rain spatters the map, falling from the sky, dripping from our faces as we bend over the map.

On our left is Great Gable. You obediently stare into thick cloud on your left. You can just distinguish where the track starts up, over patches of reddish scree. To the right of Gable is a gully, Aaron Slack; this runs up between Great Gable and Green Gable. Now for goodness' sake whatever you do never try going up Aaron Slack; you may come down it, though that is unpleasant enough, but don't go *up* it. On the map it looks like a good quick way over to Ennerdale; so in theory it is, but the gully is full of loose slack and scrambling up this is sheer punishment. Oddly enough the name, Aaron Slack, has nothing to do with slack; a *slack* here is a slight depression between two heights.

138

20 *Hunting with the Blencathra fox-hounds in Borrowdale*

At the foot of the Slack lies Sty Head Tarn, always melancholy. It is skirted by the pack-pony route which from here takes you down to Borrowdale. Above the tarn Seathwaite Fell is lost in mist. Over us rears Great End, massive with crag.

And now two figures appear, climbing up from Borrowdale; apparently two hump-backs, strangely helmeted. On drawing closer they are to be distinguished as two young men, wearing rubber-capes over their rucksacks, which accounts for the humped-back look, while on their heads are sou'-westers. They have bare, hairy, calf-bulging legs finishing in thick woollen socks, two pairs, and heavy boots. We shout 'Good morning' to one another and I add, enthusiastically, 'Isn't it lovely!' 'Aye, grand!' they call back. Neither side is being sarcastic.

The map is now put away; we must up and on. We take the track which bends to our right, upwards under Great End. The cloud grows thicker as we advance and we are completely soused, but the effort of walking steeply uphill keeps us warm and once we are used to the feeling of being wet it is not unpleasant; moreover, since one can't get any wetter one now trots along with a certain sensation of abandon. I point out that this business of getting soaked is frightfully good for one psychologically. Your reply is muffled.

Beside us runs Ruddy Ghyll, a small beck in which we appear most of the time to be walking. We are now actually upon Esk Hause. After a short distance the cloud starts shifting and blowing so that one has the sensation of walking in a landscape of moving net-curtains; suddenly there is a gleam on our left and we see the rippling of water round black, green-topped boulders; Sprinkling Tarn, as beautiful as its name. From it Grain Ghyll descends to Stockley Bridge and Borrowdale; this is a very good route to know, with a well-marked track. *Grain* means either red, or the fork of a stream; opinion conflicts as to whether this ghyll is named for some of its reddish scree, or because of its forked beck. I would think the latter.

After a brief pause on the margin of the tarn, appreciating the scraps of distant Borrowdale which appear between the cloud-curtains for a moment and then vanish again, we resume our trudge up Esk Hause. Nothing to see but rolling ground and rolling mist with an occasional boulder or sheep, the latter wearing a species of silvery aura due to the moisture caught in the wool. Saintly sheep.

141

21 *Hardrigg Ghyll, Scafell*

On we go. More wind stirs the air, the cloud is in movement all around us, disclosing patches of grey crag, little gullies full of blea-berry plants, ledges of green turf. But these glimpses are vouchsafed only for a moment; the mood of the morning is kaleidoscopic.

The ground levels out a little and becomes increasingly soggy; we have reached the top of Esk Hause and are at that spot marked on the map as *Shelter*. You would be entitled to expect a nice little hut, but there is in fact nothing more here than a battered heap of stones. Personally I think that there was once a proper shelter here, in all likelihood first built by the monks, but that since the end of the busy days of the pack trains this shelter has fallen into ruin.

Here Esk Hause is joined by two other tracks; from our left, over Glaramara and Allen Crags, an excellent and comparatively little trodden route to Thornythwaite and Borrowdale, from our right the track on to England's highest mountain peak. This is our route.

Scafell is England's greatest mountain and this way up is the classic approach over Great End and the Pikes; a well-cairned and boot-scraped approach.

'Is it far to the top?' you want to know.

'That depends entirely on which top you are talking about.'

'Why, I thought we were climbing Scafell Pike, the highest mountain in England?'

'There is no such mountain as Scafell Pike.'

'Oh, don't be so ridiculous.'

'I repeat, there is no such mountain as Scafell Pike. There is a mountain called Scafell and to this mountain is attached a chain of Pikes, or peaks. Over these Pikes we are now walking. The Pike standing next to the summit of Scafell is 3,210 feet, 48 feet higher than Scafell himself and thus the highest point in England, but nonetheless still only a part of Scafell. So, when you get back this evening and people ask you where you have been, tell them that you have been up the Pikes.'

'How desperately pedantic.'

'And another thing, I have heard you calling it Scawfell. There is no such word as scaw. Scaw means nothing. It is Scafell, pronounced Scarf'l.'

'And what pray is a sca?'

'Sca, or scar, or scarth, they are all the same thing, meaning in Norse, steep, or sheer, or crag-bound. This is a sca fell.'

I then go on to say that if it were a clear day we would now be getting a wonderful view of Great Gable. Your reply is indistinct.

All we can see is mist and the rocky ground over which our track goes. '. . . not a blade of grass is to be seen. Cushions or tufts of moss, parched and brown, appear between the huge blocks and stones that lie in heaps . . .'. This is Wordsworth describing the route over the Pikes and it is exact.

So now we are slogging along by Cold Kell Hole and Little Arra' Cove, over Ill Crag, then on to Broad Crag, upping and downing from one pike to the other, finally descending to the gully-head of Ill Rake Ghyll and then up again to the large cairn which is your Mecca. Although everything is obscured by thick cloud we are lucky that the rain is of the softer sort, falling fairly straight and not driven on the sides of a high wind. We are equally lucky not to be scorched by blazing sunshine (I hear your brittle laugh). The perfect day for the Pikes and Scafell is a cool one with high cloud; again more often encountered in the autumn, or back-end as it is here called, or in spring or the wonderful weather so often to be enjoyed in this District in the winter, although then, if there has been snow, you will need an ice-axe to ensure your safety on ice-covered slopes. In summer it is worth bearing in mind that Scafell and the surrounding big tops are more likely to be cloud-free early in the day, or late; though late fell-walking is not really to be advocated lest you are beset by darkness while still on the fells. It is the tourist business of starting the day after a latish breakfast and getting back home in time for an evening meal which bedevils so much popular fell-walking, for it means you are reaching the tops at the worst possible time of the day; the hours when they are either at their dimmest in cloud, or their most unbearable in heat.

On a clear day there is a celebrated view from the Pikes; one can see the Isle of Man, the Mourne Mountains and the Welsh hills. However, perhaps it is a little unkind of me to mention this.

We are in a place where it is not wise to wander about in a mist if you do not know your ground and I am about to suggest that I show you the way down to the so-called Guides' Route, a very useful track to know, when the mist parts, in that spectacular manner it has up here, and we find ourselves looking through what might be described as a large, jagged-framed window in the cloud, at a narrow and rocky ridge which runs from the Pike on which we are stationed to a great mass of towering rock which is the summit of Scafell himself. This gap which confronts us is Windy Gap and the narrow ridge is Mickledore. On our left the fellside swoops down towards Upper Eskdale, while below us on our right are the gullies and flanks of Lingmell. Note the lie of the land quickly, for in a few moments all will be devoured by mist again.

We scramble down to Mickledore, a descent of some ten minutes or so, cross Mickledore, which is not nearly so narrow as it looks, and find our way on to Scafell barred by a steep pitch of rock set at a very nasty angle: Broad Stand. Although Coleridge apparently negotiated this while out alone, and my father once rather astonishingly met three Lancashire gentlemen in city shoes, city suits and bowler-hats who had just successfully negotiated it, Broad Stand is a place best left to rock-climbers. Our way lies down the little scree track which dips off on our right from Mickledore.

There are three great crags of Scafell; Pikes Crag, facing south, East Buttress and Scafell Crag itself. They are all famous climbing grounds. East Buttress, to the left, immensely black and grim, like a Norman fortress, is the most formidable crag in the District. It overhangs in almost its entire length and its climbs have only been opened up in recent years, being of great severity.

Our descending track brings us on to a grass ledge below Scafell Crag; a magnificent piece of rock-architecture. For sheer strength and beauty of rock there are few places to rival this in Britain. The great buttress is the celebrated C.B. (Central Buttress) first climbed in 1914, the most difficult pitch of which is Flake Crack. The three chimneys furrowing the face of the crag are, from right to left as you face them, Deep, Steep and Moss. You are now looking at some of the great classic climbs; the Shamrock and Botterill's Slab, the Pinnacle, Pisgah, West Wall and the rest. Across the crag run two parallel rakes; the lower one, a much steadier walk than it looks, is the Lord's Rake, while the slighter rake above, running at the foot of the climbs, is the Rake's Progress. I propose getting to the top of Scafell (and you will too providing you have a steady head, intelligent feet and a zest for a little scrambling) by going along this rake and up Deep Ghyll, which is simply a very stony gully, rather than a chimney proper. Look out for stones coming down from above and make it a point that you don't dislodge any yourself. If you do, immediately warn the person following you.

There is still too much cloud for a view of anything but the immediate neighbourhood; of rock shapes and masses, a sensation of depth plunging below, the details of the valley obscured by shifting patches of cloud, so that it is rather like looking through cloud from an airplane. Occasionally comes a glimpse of the Gable, only to be lost again. You understand now why Scafell is the true summit and not the Pike; here there is a magnificence of rock and power of atmosphere that the Pike simply does not possess.

To get down we skirt somewhat leftwards to avoid the crag, picking up the Lord's Rake, which we traverse to its further end and thence drop down to Hollow Stones below. From here our route lies to our right, the famous Guides' Route, hugging the contour to cross Piers Ghyll and Greta Fall, well-marked and cairned at intervals: this invaluable route returns us finally to the First-Aid Post at Sty Head.

If you do not wish to include Mickledore and Scafell from the summit Pike, but wish to return to Sty Head in a different way from that by which you came up the Pikes, then descend into the hollow between the summit Pike and Broad Crag and drop rightwards from there down the ghyll which is the upper section, properly, of Piers Ghyll before the crags and chasms of that place begin. The beck rising amongst the stones here provides the best drinking water that thirsty walker ever found. You will pick up the Guides' Route a little below your drinking place and follow it to Sty Head.

Piers Ghyll is to be treated with marked respect always; you can look at it, cautiously, from a trod which ascends the left-hand bank of the ravine, finally connecting with the Guides' Route. It is unwise to use this route as a descent.

I imagine it will be afternoon by the time we find ourselves back at the First-Aid Post; getting on for tea-time in fact. The clouds will now lift well, the rain will have stopped, the fellsides around will be largely exposed to view, enabling you to see properly what wild and rugged country this is. It is most odd that round about tea-time, in this area of the central *massif*, the weather almost always seems to clear for a short time each day. I have noticed it again and again.

Of course one can spend years acquainting oneself thoroughly with these central fells. There is something about getting to know a mountain intimately, in detail, that is reminiscent of the process of getting to know a great painting.

Great Gable, approached from Wasdale Head, may be climbed either by the Neese or from Sty Head by that track I have already pointed out to you; the so-called easy way, which is really rather a slog. The best way up Great Gable is from Wind Gap, which lies on the north-eastern side of the mountain between Great and Green Gables. If you are proposing to climb Gable from anywhere in the District apart from Wasdale Head or Sty Head then start from Honister, taking the Drum House route of Grey Knotts, Brandreth[1] and Green Gable. There is a sharp but easy descent down a pink scree track from the top of Green Gable into the *col* from which runs Aaron Slack, then you start your ascent of Great Gable proper; a steep, scrambly but really entertaining route which is strenuous going but never deteriorates into mere slogging.

Gable boasts three great climbing grounds; the Napes Ridges and Kern Knotts to the south, and the northern precipices. The summit crags above the Napes are named the Westmorland Crags. There is a wonderful soaring view from them directly into the dark ravine of Piers Ghyll.

On the top of the mountain is a war memorial, or rather a plaque explaining that the surrounding central summits were presented to the National Trust by the Fell and Rock-Climbing Club as a memorial to their members who fell in the First World War. There is always a frightful amount of litter up here, keeping Britain untidy being a major occupation with so many people.

Great Gable is encircled by the Traverse, a high-level route which should appeal to any agile person with a head for heights and a fondness for scrambling. One really doesn't know Gable until one has done the Traverse. A clear day is desirable. The route is picked up from the Wasdale side of the Sty; it is seen leading off to the left diagonally as

[1] A brandreth was an iron tripod fixed over the fire to support a pot or kettle; Brandreth the fell is supposed to resemble such a three-legged implement.

you approach the summit of the Sty, coming up from Wasdale. It passes the foot of Kern Knotts (where, with luck, you may see climbers on the famous Crack or on the Buttress) and then rises to the screes of Great Hell Gate. You will, especially on a warm day, think this place to be appropriately named after that destination which is the opposite of Paradise, but in fact a *hell* is the old Norse for a place where water comes down; more exactly it means *to pour, to gush* (Norse, *hella*) and these scree-gullies certainly are places where it pours and gushes after heavy rain.

The Traverse crosses Great Hell Gate with Tophet Wall looming over it, then passes under the Napes Ridges. To reach the climbs you turn up a track which leads you through Needle Gully to the foot of the Needle; on your right, but you can't miss it. The Needle is officially graded as Very Difficult; the really unpleasant bit comes just below the top block and is aptly named the Mantelshelf. Imagine, if you can, climbing on to a mantelshelf, bearing in mind that it is 40 feet above the ground. Dodgy. A gingerly traverse along the Mantelshelf is followed by a climb up a face of the final block; the amount of room on the summit feels, indeed is, limited. For those to whom the original Haskett-Smith route seems too simple there are variations.

In 1828 the Needle was seen and sketched by J. W. Robinson, father of the more celebrated climbing J. W. Robinson of Whinfell Hall, Lorton. The first ascent of the Needle was not made until 1886, by W. P. Haskett-Smith, who had made the first recorded Gable climb, the Needle Ridge, two years earlier.

In these opening years British rock-climbing was mainly devoted to what Haskett-Smith called 'chimney-sweeping'; in other words most of the climbing took place in gullies, the so-called chimneys, gradually emerging from these often wet and chock-stone blocked recesses on to the open rock of the buttresses. The ascent of the Needle did more than all else to open up the sport in this country. The great names of that early climbing era on British crags appear; J. W. Robinson, W. C. Slingsby, G. Hastings, the Abraham Brothers of Keswick (to whom we also owe all those fascinating old climbing photographs), George Seatree, dear Dr Pendlebury, G. A. Solly, J. Oppenheimer, G. H. L. Mallory, F. Kennedy, J. W. F. Forbes and the rest.

Some of these men lived in the District and had week-end access to the climbs, others were professional, often university men, who had sufficient vacation time in which to climb seriously. These were leisurely, moneyed days; gentlemanly, with much practical joking of the sort Victorians delighted in. Mountain *mystique* had a strong public-school flavour; nobody would have been seen dead wearing today's red socks, green knickerbockers or orange anoraks; indeed anoraks were not discovered. Of course everyone climbed in nails.

The live-wire of these days was a highly gymnastic young man named Owen Glynne Jones, who was first stimulated to visit the Lake District by a photograph of the Needle displayed in a window of the Strand. A fortnight later it was Easter, Jones was on his way to Wasdale Head and in no time was perched on the top of his goal.

A slim, bespectacled man, he was full of daring innovations and variations and a trifle impatient of tradition; rock-climbing has always been a great sport for battles between traditional attitudes and new. At Wasdale Head I once met an elderly woman who as a girl had climbed with Glynne Jones; she recounted how he was not above performing singularly delicate passages of rock-ballet wearing socks over his boots, which apparently shook the Old Guard. It should be noted here that rope was not used in climbing until the 1880's; this the earliest purists decried as an unnatural aid as vehemently as today's purists deplore 'artificial'.[1]

The centre for these climbers was the hotel at Wasdale Head. Many are the anecdotes of the hotel in these days and I count myself lucky that I have known people who have been able to tell these tales at first hand. The high-spirited company, restored by dinner following a hard day climbing on Gable, Scafell or Pillar, would experiment with hotel routes, both outside the premises (Stable Door Traverse) and inside (Billiard Room Traverse, Billiard Table Hand Traverse). Fives were also played in the billiard-room. When one tired of this there was, a short distance up Mosedale (indeed still is) a boulder up which several necessarily short but esoteric routes were devised, including one which must always be done feet foremost.

There are memories of the big chest which was kept full of discarded

[1] The modern technique for climbing overhanging faces: artificial stances are contrived by *pitons* driven into the rock; from the *piton* the climber then suspends himself by a minute *étrier* (stirrup) and thus suspended hammers in the next *piton*, and so on.

148

22 *Pikes Crag: grooved arête route*

23 (right) *Ennerdale Water*

24   *Ennerdale, from Green Gable. Pillar and Pillar Rock on left*

or lost clothing; if one arrived without a second pullover, say, or a spare pair of socks one went to this chest and rummaged in it to see if one could discover a replacement. One highly distinguished Cambridge man, of exceptionally absent mind, left a tweed jacket behind. On coming up to Wasdale Head at Easter he remarked that he had forgotten to bring a jacket with him, went to the chest and shortly afterwards appeared wearing his own jacket, observing that he had found this jacket which seemed to fit him admirably: 'Good fortune to place my hands on something so exactly measured to my own build.' At the end of his stay he dutifully returned the jacket to the Treasure Chest.

Another agreeable custom, common also to Burnthwaite Farm, was that climbers tossed their wet clothes at the end of the day in a large heap on the landing outside the bedrooms. In the morning everyone rushed from their rooms to delve in the pile of dried clothes which had now materialised. The confusion amongst socks was considerable.

One of the characters most affectionately handed down to us from those days was Owd Joe, a shepherd. He was the delight of all who went to Wasdale and many are the stories about him. One of the most famous tells of the time that Joe, excited by strong drink, burst into a strange tongue which was identified by some intellectual visitor as Icelandic. Joe had never spoken Icelandic in his life before, neither was he to do so again. I must confess that I have always suspected that Joe, a true Cumbrian, excelled at the subtle art of leg-pulling.

A popular item on the programme at shepherds' meets (of which more, later) is the contest in which the prize goes to the man who can pull the worst faces. Joe, it is claimed, won first prize, only for it to be discovered that he had in fact not been taking part in the contest but following the proceedings 'with sympathy and interest' as an onlooker.

There are scores of good Joe stories. I would much like to hear some of Joe's stories about the climbers. Still waters run deep and Cumbrian waters are among the deepest.

But we are still at the foot of the Needle; to the left of the Needle gully is the Eagle's Nest gully and the left wall of this gully is the Arrowhead Ridge. These climbs are particularly popular because they are on quick-drying granite; Gable is a granite mountain. From these gullies we return on to the Traverse which now crosses Little Hell Gate and swings round the south-west corner of the mountain, the

25 *Catbells and Derwentwater, from Maiden Moor*

gable, or gavel, itself. From thence the Traverse follows a rough but open passage to Beck Head, the *col* between Great Gable and Kirkfell. Kirkfell is little explored; one can spend an entire afternoon wandering about its enormous top without seeing a soul, even in the high season. Friends who have accompanied me up there assure me that the solitude I so much enjoy there is due to the fact that no sane person would wish to spend the afternoon roaming about on Kirkfell.

A conspicuous boulder will be noticed just before the track up the Neese, from Wasdale, joins the Traverse. This boulder is Moses's Finger. We are now approaching Gable Crag, the north face of the mountain, where rock-climbers are joined by the shade of a very mysterious personality.

The Traverse takes you round the base of the Gable Crag, mostly narrow scree-track to follow, bringing you out by the *col* between Great Gable and Green Gable. The Doctor's Chimney I have mentioned earlier is some distance up one of the most westerly scree gullies; no wonder that the doctor's dog disliked this expedition. Gable Crag is not so easily accessible as either Kern Knotts or the Napes Ridges, consequently although it harbours some wonderful climbs, many of them of severity, it is not nearly such a popular climbing-ground.

The Boat Howe Crags on the Ennerdale side of Kirkfell were opened up by Graham Brown in 1925 and the climbs were given nautical names of considerable ingenuity: Coastguard Climb, Sea Wall Arête, Breakwater Slabs and Lighthouse, Hatchway and Rigging, Larboard Arête, Starboard Chimney and the like. There may be some truth in the allegation that climbers are people who never grow up, though whether this is a fault or a virtue I must leave with the reader to decide.

But now you want to know who Moses was; Moses, whose finger-rock we have passed, marking the route known as Moses's Sledgate, or Sledgait, which runs from the Neese to Beck Head, from thence following the contours of Gable's northern flanks to cross the infant River Liza rising below Wind Gap, then Tongue Beck and so on to Brandreth and Honister.

Moses, according to legend, was a smuggler who, some say, conveyed his contraband from Wasdale Head (whence it had come from Ravenglass) up the Neese and on to his Sledgate, hauling it, as the name implies, on a wooden sledge of the sort still used by Cumbrian farmers and in the old days also used by quarrymen. Whether Moses himself pulled the sledge or whether he used a pony nobody seems to have decided. The track is an excellent, contour-hugging one apart from that first awful pull up Gable Neese. But why did Moses wish to haul contraband from Wasdale Head to Honister?

H. H. Symonds has a convincing theory. He suggests that Moses was a quarryman from the Honister slate-quarries who smuggled wadd as a sideline. The contour-hugging Sledgate, or Moses's Trod as it is sometimes also called, certainly supports this theory; as Symonds points out, quarrymen were adept at creating quarry-roads which, by sticking to a contour, avoided unnecessary exertion. From Honister, continues the expert, it was easy-going to the wadd, or plumbago, mines in Borrowdale and during the eighteenth century, when Borrowdale wadd was at a premium, smuggling of the substance was extremely profitable. Therefore Moses pulled his sled of wadd along his Trod and down the Neese (not up), possibly handing the stuff over, at Wasdale Head, to black-marketeers in the valuable wadd: a pony-pack of wadd was worth about £800.

This certainly seems convincing. Wasdale legend has it, however, that Moses was a whisky-distiller, a moonshiner.

A further mystery in this tale is the ruined stone hut which squats at the top of Central Gully on the Gable Crag and which was first discovered by J. W. Robinson about 1890. The roof of this hut long since disappeared, but the walls, though damaged, still stand and although it does not look as if whisky were ever distilled there on the other hand the hut seems clearly to have been a hide-out for something or somebody. It is not a shepherd's hut. It can only be gained by a stiff scramble; it is a wonderful look-out position. Graham Sutton once suggested that it was perhaps a hideout for the Derwentwater Radcliffes who were deeply involved in the '15 Rebellion, but there was no reason, it seems to me, why the Radcliffes should have used a hideout in this particular place.

Whisky or wadd would seem the likeliest explanation for this hut where, Sutton has told us, he used to climb to smoke a contemplative pipe and where I in my turn used to go in my romantically disposed youth to write poetry. It would be interesting to know how many writers have used this retreat. It would be even more interesting to know precisely what old Moses did there.

I assume that there was a Moses because such vivid traditions as this one is usually have factual roots. That there was a thriving wadd-smuggling trade we certainly know. Moses must have been a strong man to have hauled a sledge along his Trod, even stronger to have built this hut, if indeed he built it. Yet someone built it. And the mind boggles at the thought of erecting a stone hut in such a position. How were the stones assembled? The walls were of dry-stone; one wonders what the roof was made of. Not of slate, certainly.

But the Honister quarrymen were of formidable strength, as is demonstrated by that passage in E. Lynn Linton's guidebook where she describes a visit to the quarry: 'This slate quarrying is awful to look at, both in the giddy height at which the men work, and in the terrible journeys which they make when bringing down the slate in their "sleds". It is simply appalling to see that small moving speck on the high crag, passing noiselessly along a narrow grey line that looks like a mere thread, and to know that it is a man with the chances of his life dangling in his hand. As we look the speck moves; he first crosses the straight gallery leading out from the dark cavern where he emerged and then he sets himself against the perpendicular descent, and comes down the face of the crag, carrying something behind him—at first slowly, and as it were, cautiously; then with a swifter step, but still evidently holding back; but at the last with a wild haste that seems as if he must be overtaken, and crushed to pieces by the heavy sled grinding after him. The long swift steps seem almost to fly; the noise of the crashing slate comes nearer; now we see the man's eager face; and now we hear his panting breath; and now he draws up by the road-side—every muscle strained, every nerve alive, and every pulse throbbing with frightful force. It is a terrible trade—and the men employed in it look wan and worn, as if they were all consumptive or had heart disease. The average daily task is seven or eight of these journeys, carrying about a quarter of a ton of slate each time; the downward run occupying only a few minutes, the return climb—by another path not quite so perpendicular, where they crawl with their empty sleds on their backs, like some strange beetle or fly—half an hour. Great things used to be done in former times, and the quarrymen still talk of Samuel Trimmer, who once made 15 journeys in one day, for the reward of a small percentage on the hurdle and a bottle of rum; and of Joseph Clark, a Stonethwaite man, who brought down 42½ loads, or 10,880 lbs. of slate, in 17 journeys; travelling 17 miles— eight and a half up the face of the crag, and the same number down, at this murderous pace. These are almost legendary days. . . . Twelve journeys a day rank now as a feat scarcely to be compassed; for no man of modern slate-quarrying powers can do anything near to these giants of the elder time.'

Mrs Linton was writing in 1864. She goes on to add that 'the quarry-men have small sleeping huts among the crags, and remain during the week at their work, going home only from the Saturday night to the Monday morning . . .'.

Thus, if Moses were a quarryman, we realise that pulling a sled round his Sledgate would have been nothing more than a little mild exercise at the end of the day.

Moses's Trod may also be gained from a track out of the head of Ennerdale which, contour-hugging like the Trod, links up with the Pillar High Level Route, the climbers' way to Pillar Rock. This High Level Route was discovered by J. W. Robinson and is perhaps the best walk in the entire District for those who love sensations of space and intimate views of the mountains. One starts from Looking Stead, which one reaches either from Black Sail or by the route mentioned above. Drop westwards a little from Looking Stead, then start mounting the rise towards Pillar, keeping the remains of an old iron fence on your right. After, say, a hundred yards of uphill work you will see, on your right beyond the disintegrating fence, a large cairn on a rock: it marks the commencement of the High Level Route.

I have heard people give frightful accounts of this route; in fact it is perfectly safe for anyone with a sound head for heights and normally sure-footed. It is really a sheep-trod, marked at intervals by tall, cone-shaped cairns. The last, extra large one is Robinson's Cairn, erected to him as a memorial under the direction of Haskett-Smith. There is a memorial tablet nearby.

Robinson made his first ascent of Pillar Rock in 1882. He was not only a pioneer of rock-climbing but also a prodigious walker, once, in 1893, walking 70 miles in 24 hours, covering the principal tops.

Baddeley gives details of his route: 'Keswick, Great Gable, Scafell (by Pikes Traverse from Skew Gill and Deep Gill, West Wall Traverse), Scafell Pikes (*via* Broad Stand), Great End, Bowfell, Langdale Combe Head, Wythburn, Helvellyn, Saddleback, Skiddaw. Abandoned on Skiddaw. Time, 23 hours 25 minutes.' This is not the record: Dr Wakefield in 1905 walked 90 miles, the equivalent of 120, in 22 hours 7 minutes. Ascents, 23,500 feet. Later Mr E. Thomas, coached by the doctor, knocked this time down to 21 hours 25 minutes. You will find detailed accounts of record fell-walks in the Baddeley guide; they make exhausting reading.

The Rock, most famous of all rocks in climbing history, is like a magnificent gothic structure. It consists of two towers, as it were, fused together; the one higher than the other. They are named High Man and Low Man. The rock which joins, or appears to join, High Man to Pillar Mountain is called Shamrock, or the Sham Rock, and an eastern gully, Walker's Gully, separates Sham Rock and High Man. The gullies, with which Pillar Rock is scarred, create an impression of fluted pillars. Westwards, to the left of High Man, lies the Jordan Gap and to the left again of Jordan Gap is Pisgah. There is not time for me to detail here what might be termed a Scrambler's Guide to Pillar Rock, but Symonds gives an excellent one which you should study closely if you are interested in making a tour of this natural cathedral. I would only observe that there is a track up on to the fell by either side of the Rock and that both the scree-funnels which flank the Rock on either side degenerate into dangerously rock-bound lower reaches.

In the old days the Rock was known as Pillar Stone. The first recorded ascent was on July 9th 1826 by one John Atkinson, a shepherd or a cooper (nobody is certain which) of Croftfoot, Ennerdale. In that same year a party of shepherds followed his example. The next recorded ascent was not until 22 years later, when Lieut. Wilson of the Royal Navy enlivened a shore-leave by climbing the Rock. Other parties followed. By 1876 some 120 recorded ascents had been made. The first woman to triumph over the Rock was Miss A. Barker who climbed it in 1870.

On to the scene now comes one of those doughty Victorians of whom it can be truly said that they do not come like that any more: the Rev. 'Steeple' Jackson, so-called because he had once climbed up his own church-spire at Rivington to repair the weather-cock, the professional local steeplejacks having refused the job. Jackson was a great one for writing short commemorative verses about himself and on this occasion produced:

Who has not heard of Steeple Jack
That lion-hearted Saxon?
Though I'm not he, he was my sire
For I am Steeple Jackson.

Jackson was a great walker; in his sixty-ninth year he walked 46 miles in 14½ hours, two days later he walked 56 miles in 18 hours, and after another two days he achieved 60 miles in less than 20 hours. When the old gentleman, in his eightieth year, heard that women were climbing Pillar Rock he could not restrain himself and on May 31st 1875 with a companion of somewhat more youthful years, he climbed the Rock. On the summit he deposited a bottle with a message in it:

If this in your mind you will fix
When I make the Pillar my toy,
I was born in 1, 7, 9, 6,
And you'll think me a nimble old boy.

The self-styled Patriarch of the Pillarites in the following year made a solo ascent; two years later, in 1878, he set out to make another solo attempt. He did not return from his expedition and was found by a search-party lying dead in Great Doup Cove, close by the Rock. He had not fallen from the Rock; it is possible he had simply collapsed. He was, after all, 82. There is a memorial to him in the Cove.

The history of climbing on the Rock follows the history of the sport in general; first the gullies were climbed, moving from thence on to more exposed pitches, the routes becoming increasingly severe. The Rock is now climbed in all directions and provides some of the severest routes in the country, as well as some easy ways such as the happy old Slab-and-Notch.

From the summit of the Rock one gets a wonderful view of Ennerdale; once, some 30 years ago now, a barren sheep-grazed valley, not thick with afforestation as it is today. May I hasten to say that my earliest memories of Ennerdale do not extend to the treeless days, though I can recall the trees when they were, so to speak, in their childhood.

At the bottom of Ennerdale winds the River Liza; a name, Collingwood suggests, that is derived from the same source as that from which the Icelandic river Lysa derives, meaning 'bright water'. He goes on to tell us that this is the district of Copeland (*Kaupa-land*, a bought land, i.e. not inherited), true Icelandic territory still.

The Old Guard deplored the planting of Ennerdale with conifers, forgetting, one feels, that a barren Ennerdale such as they were used to and hated to see spoiled was, in fact, unnatural. Ennerdale, until the sixteenth century, was forest-filled, as all these Lakeland valleys were, although it was northern deciduous forest and therefore less monotonous than coniferous forest. Perhaps next time that Ennerdale is planted deciduous spinneys will be included to break the evergreen.

There is not time for me to take you walking on the fells of Ennerdale, which is a pity, but I must suggest to you that you try not to miss the wonderful day that awaits you should you decide to walk the Red Pike, Scoatfell, Steeple, Windy Gap and Pillar ridge which embraces the head of Mosedale and is one of the finest ridge walks in the District. The Buttermere Fells, which lie facing Pillar, across Ennerdale, are best explored from Buttermere. To get to Buttermere from Ennerdale you go by Scarth Gap, above the lonely Youth Hostel hut, or there is a longer way, further westwards, by little-known Floutern (*flow*-tarn, the tarn of the bog, a most apt name).

A friend of mine tells me that, while walking from Ennerdale to Buttermere by this route, she found, on the highest and driest part of the track, a mass of frog-spawn. She could not conceive how it had got there. The fact is that when one discovers either frog or toad-spawn lying on an exposed upland track one may be quite certain that a fox has carried it there; the animals greatly enjoy it, no doubt it is their equivalent of caviare.

We must now return to Wasdale Head, for it is time to travel to Keswick and Borrowdale. If you are touring on foot you will go over the Sty to Borrowdale from Wasdale; the classic route. This has been a pedestrians' chapter; how could it be otherwise when only those who go on foot can explore the central *massif* of fells? The best things in life must still be sweated after.

You in your car, or now returned to your car after bravely traipsing around with me, will choose perhaps to drive to Keswick by what may be described as a perimeter road, from Strands to Calder Bridge, thence to Egremont, Cleator, Ennerdale Bridge (perhaps taking time to drive out of your way to see Ennerdale Water), then on to Lamplugh and from thence to Lowes Water, from there to Lorton and by the Whin-latter Pass over to pretty little Braithwaite and Keswick reposing under Skiddaw. You will see, in this way, the coastline of atomic power-station and coalfields which is as much an integral part of Cumberland as Scafell. But if you wish to go to Keswick by a more romantic and undoubtedly more beautiful way, though this Calder Bridge–Cleator Moor way has a grey and windswept beauty of its own, then you will return to Grasmere and take the road over Dunmail Raise, by Wythburn and Thirlmere.

CHAPTER NINE

The Heart of the Matter: Keswick, Borrowdale, Buttermere

Traffic moves constantly over Dunmail Raise in the season, leaving one with little chance to brood upon the shades which people this historic thoroughfare. The first identifiable personality to appear is Chief Dunmail, a character who presents himself to our imagination, wrongly perhaps, but inevitably, in the guise of an Old Vic actor, wielding a heavy sword and yelling defiance. He is surrounded by his Cumbrian supporters; lesser chiefs and warriors, assisting him to resist a punitive raid which Edmund, King of the Saxons, and his ally, Malcolm of Scotland, are carrying out against the land of Cumbria. The year is A.D. 945 or thereabouts and the figures are obscured both by the mists of time and weather. They race about the fellsides, dodge amongst the boulders. The clashing of swords and hoarse shouting echo in our ears; Cumbria is defeated, Dunmail is taken prisoner. Legend claims he was killed and buried under a large cairn of which the remains can still be seen, but historical fact shows that he was captured, to survive the battle by some 30 years or so, dying at last in Rome where he had gone on a pilgrimage. The Saxon king gave Cumbria to Malcolm, as a reward for his part in the struggle.

Now come centuries of travellers; monks, wool-merchants, farmers, tinkers, peddlars, poets, passing over the Raise, back and forth between Ambleside and Keswick. In the late eighteenth and the nineteenth centuries we hear the grind, clatter and clink of the horse-coaches; the four-in-hands, with the coachmen blowing the signal of their approach on their yards-of-tin, as their long coach horns were called. These four-in-hands survived into the first quarter of the twentieth century, competing with the first rattling and uncomfortable motor-charabancs, but once the roads were surfaced the horses were hopelessly handi-capped. Horses cannot keep back a laden coach on a hard smooth sur-face with a gradient of one-in-four-and-a-half behind them.

The Lakeland coachmen were renowned. Affectionately named 'coachees' they developed a style of anecdote and repartee which made them the Victorian equivalent of today's New York taxi-drivers. They worked long hours in all weathers, especially the mail-coach drivers, with whom it was a point of honour that the mail must always go through. Richard Rigg's coaches held the mail-contract between Windermere and Grasmere; he dressed his drivers in red coats. Most of the coachees wore white top-hats and otter-skin gloves, the latter always a favourite with coachmen. Old people in the District speak lovingly of the four-in-hands.

Two tales of the old horse-coaches may perhaps find room here; one is of Wordsworth (who always looked much older than his actual years) travelling on a coach with a talkative group of passengers, including a chirrupy old gentleman who, after listening to the conver-sation for a while, turned to Wordsworth and remarked, 'Ah, they'll be talking differently when they're our age, won't they?' 'Our age? Why, how old do you think I am?' asked the poet. 'About the same as mine; getting on for seventy', said the old gentleman. 'I am thirty-nine', was the Wordsworthian rejoinder.

The other tale, often repeated but worth repeating again since it may well be new for some readers and it demonstrates the pithy attitude of the coachees, relates how a coachman who was keeping up an informative running commentary for the benefit of his tourist passen-gers became increasingly annoyed by a German lady who was spoiling his stories with her constant interruptions. As they approached Helm Crag, in the silhouette of which one is supposed to be able to discern (among other things) a Lion and a Lamb, the German exclaimed, 'But Helm Crag, coachman, with Lion and Lamb; I never see the Lamb but only the Lion.' 'Mum, that there's a British Lion you see; and the Lamb is now inside, ate while you were coming up the pass.'

If we were travelling to Keswick by leisurely coach there would be plenty of time to regale you with information concerning the route, but we travel too fast these days; we whirl past Wythburn, past Thirlmere, now a mesmerised and semi-artificial lake, a Manchester Corporation Reservoir, past Naddle Fell and Castlerigg. But if we can find time we should deviate from the road at Castlerigg to visit the celebrated Bronze Age stone circle.

Then on to Keswick, lying between Skiddaw and Derwentwater. Here, in A.D. 553, arrived the Christian St Kentigern, also known as St Mungo, engaged upon mission work amongst what were then pagan native tribes. He set up a Cross and started preaching at Crosfeld and here a small chapel was built by his converts and dedicated to him.

Crosfeld is the English name; the Norse, when they arrived, renamed it Crosthwaite. There is still a church upon this ancient site.

About a century after St Kentigern's founding of the church of Crosthwaite there arrived another saint in the neighbourhood, St Herbert, all set upon being a hermit and looking for somewhere really lonely and uncomfortable to install himself. According to the records of the Venerable Bede he chose an island on Derwentwater; this today is known as St Herbert's Island. St Herbert was a devoted friend of St Cuthbert of Lindisfarne and long after St Herbert's death the monks of Lindisfarne made pilgrimages to the hermit-saint's island, probably being ferried across to it from that little point now celebrated as the beauty-spot of Friar's Crag. Near Portinscale there has been found the site of what might be termed a pilgrims' souvenir-shop; here crosses and probably saintly relics were on sale to pilgrims; a Lourdes-like picture.

St Kentigern's infant church was rebuilt in the twelfth century by Alice de Romilli, Lady of Allerdale. In 1198 Richard Cœur de Lion gave the rectory to Fountains Abbey, which established a grange of monks nearby (Monks Hall). The church was rebuilt in the reign of Mary Tudor and to this time date back the church's famous consecration crosses. The building was almost completely restored in 1844, but parts of the twelfth-century building still survive.

Among the earliest monuments in the church are brasses to Sir John

26 *Moot Hall, Keswick*

Radcliffe and his wife Dame Alice. Sir John led a contingent of Keswick men to the Battle of Flodden Field, but lived nevertheless to die peacefully at his family home on Lord's Island, Derwentwater. Dame Alice, who survived him a number of years, is buried in Salisbury Cathedral. The Radcliffes, during the reign of Henry VI, married into the Derwentwater family; one of the District's oldest families. The Derwentwater-Radcliffes made a fortune out of mine-owning during the reign of James I and were created Earls of Derwentwater during the reign of James II. Naturally the family was Jacobite in its loyalties and the last Earl, James, was deeply involved in the 1715 Rebellion. He was taken prisoner at Preston on November 13th 1715, and the following month, together with other captured ringleaders of the Rebellion, he was marched through the streets of London to the Tower. He was executed on Tower Hill early in the New Year. The family estates were settled upon Greenwich Hospital by Act of Parliament; and that was the end of the Derwentwaters.

The font at Crosthwaite church was presented, in the fourteenth century, by Lady Derwentwater and Lady Maude, wife of the first Earl of Northumberland, as a tribute to the vicar, Sir Thomas de Eskhead.

Probably the best-known of all Crosthwaite's incumbents was Canon Rawnsley, one of the chief creators, in 1895, of the National Trust. He has no font to his memory, but Friar's Crag, Lord's Island and part of Great Wood were given to the National Trust as a living monument to him.

Crosthwaite church's most interesting feature is probably the bell-tower with its names and portraits of past bell-ringers, its list of bell-ringers' rules, its records of bell-ringing triumphs, both past and contemporary. The graveyard too is beautiful, with its wonderful views and interesting graves, including that of Southey, Poet Laureate and brother-in-law of Coleridge.

The pilgrims long ago stopped visiting St Herbert's Island, but every year crowds flock to modern Keswick for the Convention, first held in 1875 to 'promote practical holiness'. People travel from far and wide to this Convention, although it lasts now only for a week whereas it used to be for ten days. One rather odd result of Keswick's history of practical holiness is that, over the century, the town has accumulated a

27 *Skiddaw*

terminal moraine of collected sermons. The boarding-houses of Keswick must have abounded in these volumes which are now finding their way to jumble-sales and auction-rooms where they are sold in lots. I once at an auction bought a wheelbarrow full of books for half-a-crown; my haul, when examined, consisted almost exclusively of collected sermons. I suspect that these books were not in fact purchased by the boarding-house keepers of Keswick, but were presented to the good ladies by the clergymen-authors themselves, as a parting gift at the close of their Convention stay.

Keswick's most interesting literary associations concern the Coleridge–Southey *ménage* of Greta Hall. Coleridge, with his wife and little son, Hartley, came to live at the Hall in 1800, renting part of the house from its owner, William Jackson, who had made a fortune out of carting and was so delighted to have a literary philosopher as tenant that he charged Coleridge a very low rent and in the first six months no rent at all. 'A more truly disinterested man I never met with. . . . He is one instance, among many in this country, of the salutary effect of the love of knowledge', wrote the delighted philosopher in a letter. In 1803 Southey and his wife (Mrs Coleridge's sister) moved in to Greta Hall too and the family party was further swelled by Aunt Lovell, so that Southey was soon calling the house 'The Aunt Hill'. But by degrees Coleridge's marriage fell apart, the philosopher could not face the rigours and obligations of daily life. 'The moment anything assumed the shape of a duty Coleridge felt incapable of discharging it', observed Southey, who was no poet, although he became Poet Laureate, but a writer of excellent prose which fortunately proved profitable, for soon Coleridge wandered off leaving Southey to bring up both the Coleridge family and his own. It was lucky that Southey loved children.

Southey, tall, lanky, a keen walker and hard worker, was a reserved man, very shy and sensitive, but with a great sense of the comic. He was never on very good terms with Wordsworth; possibly because he found William funny and William did not like being laughed at, however goodnaturedly. Southey has left us an hilarious account of the occasion when, after the Battle of Waterloo, his family, the Wordsworths, some neighbourly friends and other less exalted persons climbed Skiddaw to light a victory bonfire. Both rum and water were carried to the summit (in separate containers) in order that Wellington and his victorious soldiers might be suitably toasted. But Wordsworth, the teetotaller of the party and always a very clumsy man (except when ice-skating, when he was unexpectedly graceful), kicked over the water. Southey then got the party to gather round Wordsworth to punish him by singing, 'Twas *you* that kicked the kettle down! 'twas you sir, you!' What water that was left was served with the rum of the gentry; the lesser mortals drank theirs neat, with the result that, 'All our torches were lit at once . . . and our way down the hill was marked by a track of fire . . .'. In short the expedition ended in unplanned rowdyism; raucous singing, shouting and one man riding down Skiddaw back-to-front on a pony.

Keswick became an established part of the Lakeland Tour, with its obligatory sights and excursions. Says Ackermann, 'Most tourists ascend Skiddaw . . . and [it] may be easily travelled either on foot or on horseback. . . . Even a lady may safely ride to the top, if in the very highest parts someone manages the horse's head.'

Skiddaw, in former times, had a hermit. He appeared, suddenly, one summer in the early 1860's, from where nobody knew. It was the shepherds who discovered him; they had noticed that a deserted hut on the fellside showed signs of occupation, but they could not catch sight of the person who was living in it. Then, unexpectedly, they came across him in a ghyll, painting a picture of a waterfall, 'an' a fine picter it was hooiver'. But they couldn't get the artist to tell them anything about himself. He lived on the fell for some time, leaving one back-end, as mysteriously as he had come. Shortly before he left he had given one shepherd-acquaintance a bit of blue slate with a grey sheep painted on it, 'but I lost it on t' fell'.

The hermit is reputed to have painted several portraits of local people, but they seem to have become untraceable; or do they turn up from time to time, unidentified, in Keswick and Cockermouth sale-rooms?

George Smith the man called himself; an alias, one strongly suspects. It is thought that he came from a respectable Banffshire family and was born about 1825. After he left Skiddaw he reappeared in southern Lakeland, becoming a familiar figure at Ambleside. He was noted for his fervent chapel-going and finally his religious mania made it necessary for him to be placed in a Banffshire asylum, where he died in 1873. Ruskin, it would seem, took an interest in this man.

Supposing Smith's paintings (of no account in his lifetime) were suddenly rediscovered and acclaimed as the works of a genius! What would the dealers not give, then, for that bit of blue slate with a grey sheep painted on it!

A hundred years ago Keswick must have been a tranquil spot. Across this gentle scene pass certain figures who especially intrigue us; the first being the distinguished geologist, Jonathan Otley, who died at Keswick in 1855, aged 90. Otley, a close friend of Professor Sedgwick and by all accounts a most delightful individual was, among other things, author of the first really reliable guide to the District and of the first accurate map. But his pet hobby throughout the greater part of his life was measuring the summer levels of Derwentwater, marking these on stones below Friar's Crag, where they may still be seen when the Lake is low. Otley did this marking annually between 1824, a very dry summer, until the even drier summer of 1852, when he was 87. One likes to visualise him, an old man carrying a tall stick, happily and slowly walking down to Friar's Crag on a hot summer evening to record yet another of his cherished water levels. And a Friar's Crag that was a place of solitude, even in midsummer!

The other Keswick personalities who especially fascinate are the makers of musical-stones. The invaluable Postlethwaite is informative about these odd instruments, which seem to have been peculiar to Keswick. The stones, he tells us, were made of 'a hard, massive, foliated and sonorous rock . . . called Spotted (or Andalusite) Schist . . .'.[1] The inventor of musical-stone instruments was Peter Crosthwaite, of Monks Hall, who made his instrument in the year 1785. It consisted of 16 stones that had been split and hammered into shape and tune. Crosthwaite exhibited it in a small museum which he had enterprisingly opened as a tourist attraction. Ackermann mentions this museum in his Tour.

Crosthwaite's stones started a fashion. To quote Postlethwaite again: 'About the year 1840, Mr Joseph Richardson, a builder, of Applethwaite, near Keswick, who possessed musical ability of a high order, was impressed by the musical sounds emitted by some of the

[1] *Mines and Mining in the Lake District.*

stone amongst which he worked, and, having, in all probability, seen and heard Peter Crosthwaite's instrument . . . set to work and constructed an elaborate instrument consisting of upwards of 70 musical stones, varying from six inches to four feet in length, the compass being nearly six octaves. But in order to produce a fuller and deeper volume of sound he added to his musical stones about 40 Swiss bells, hung upon steel bars, and tuned to the notes of the stones, and to these he added drums; the stones, bells and drums being struck by wooden mallets, by three performers, Messrs. Joseph Richardson & Sons. These men travelled with this remarkable instrument through Britain and had the honour of performing three times before Queen Victoria at Buckingham Palace.'

These are command performances one wishes one could have attended.

The Keswick craze for musical-stones did not stop with the Richardsons; in 1875 another Keswickian, Mr William Till, together with his son William 'turned their attention to music in stone, and after devoting nearly the whole of their available leisure time for about ten years, produced a fine instrument . . .' says Postlethwaite. With this instrument Mr Till, his two sons and two daughters toured Britain and afterwards the United States, giving concerts of instrumental and vocal music.

Keswick yet had more to come: 'After the departure of the Till family to America, Mr G. P. Abraham, of Keswick, and his two sons, following their example, formed an excellent instrument of the same kind. . . . Messrs. Abraham & Sons occasionally gave concerts in various large towns in Britain, in winter, but their instrument is always in evidence in Keswick during the latter part of the Tourist Season. All visitors to Keswick in the month of August should avail themselves of the opportunity of hearing the delightful music produced by Messrs. Abraham & Sons, from what I believe is the only set of Musical Stones now in use in Great Britain.'[1]

Musical Stones are on display, today, at the Keswick Museum; a place well worth a visit. It is in the upper part of the town, near the station.

Keswick has changed greatly, especially in the last few years. New

[1] Postlethwaite.

cafés, shops and restaurants have opened, the old billiard-rooms have closed, even Abrahams' have modernised the style of their hallowed window-displays, about which some old-timers are heard complaining bitterly. But change is inevitable. I have no doubt there was much complaint when the monks stopped coming to Keswick on their pilgrimages. 'We shan't get those charming old monks coming here any more; what a pity! Keswick will be sadly altered.'

And so, in fact, it soon was. Incredible as it may now seem, in Elizabethan times the district about Keswick was the contemporary Yukon and Keswick was the Dawson City of the age.

Mining prospectors appeared, prowled the valleys, returned south with favourable reports, favourable enough to get some extremely hard-headed people interested; namely Queen Elizabeth and some of her noblemen business tycoons. In 1561 the Mines-Royal Company was formed, with the Queen as Patron and the Earl of Northumberland, Lord of the Manor in which the mines lay, and Lord Burghley as leading shareholders. It was decided to place the actual mining in the hands of Bavarian experts, Bavaria being the most advanced mining area in Europe at the time. In 1562 Daniel Hechstetter and Thomas Thurland from Augsburg received a warrant from the Queen to open up the mines and to bring to England several hundred miners to work them.

The busiest mining area was the Newlands valley, west of Derwentwater. Newlands had been known as a place rich in copper ore since the time of Henry III at least, possibly long before that, but the Germans now opened up the old mines, the chief of which was one so rich in ore that the Germans named it 'Gottsgab' or God's Gift, which over the years has become Anglicised as 'Goldscope'. Besides copper, gold and silver were found in this mine, silver in quite large quantities, whereupon the Queen started a lawsuit against the Earl of Northumberland, making exclusive claim to the richer minerals, saying that the royal metals belonged to her alone while the baser (by which she meant the copper) belonged to the Earl. Of course Her Majesty won the case.

Smelting-works were built at Brigham on the outskirts of Keswick by the Greta. The forests of oak, holly and ash which clothed the lower fellsides were cut down to provide fuel for the smelting-works, the wood being burned into charcoal. Woodcutters and charcoal-burners, besides the German miners, descended upon the fells; lumber-camps were set up, the dales echoed to the sound of axes striking wood, branches crackling, saws rasping, men shouting. The charcoal-burners had their own little camps in the clearings, from which rose columns of smoke from the wigwam-like charcoal-kilns. Teams of pack-ponies carried the copper-ore from Newlands to the western shore of Derwentwater where it was taken by boat to Keswick.

The town became crowded and bustling, pack-pony trains were always passing and repassing through the streets, the inns were full of travellers, while the miners, having nowhere else to amuse themselves, came tumbling into Keswick to enjoy ale, song and wenches, with some good brawling in the streets afterwards.

There was, of course, much complaint about the behaviour of the miners. Indeed so much resentment was nurtured against them that at one point they had to be lodged on Derwent Island for their safety. Gradually, however, things settled down; many of the men married local girls (though this again caused resentment) and thus a Bavarian strain was introduced into the Keswick bloodstream, for when their contracts expired many of these miners chose to remain in the district. Perhaps this may at least in part account for Keswick's elusive atmosphere of the Tyrol which so many visitors notice and comment upon.

According to Robinson's *Natural History of Westmorland and Cumberland*[1] the Germans opened up and worked 11 veins in Newlands, including several at Dale Head. This Dale Head mine was later worked by the Duke of Somerset, who erected furnaces in the valley bottom. It is not certain whether the Germans worked the Brandley, or Brandelhow Mine, though this is certainly ancient, having been stope-and-feather worked before the use of gunpowder.

This great mining boom lasted for just on a century. The smelting-works, with their 'forcible steam, and other ingenious inventions' were destroyed by Cromwell's troops; most of the miners were either killed or drafted into Cromwell's Army. But the boom had in truth been flagging before that, simply for lack of furnace fuel. Each ton of ore smelted consumed a half-acre of trees; no wonder that the fells were, within that century of hectic mining, almost totally denuded of forest! Coal was tried as fuel instead of charcoal, but was not successful.

[1] Published 1709.

The Yukon-like element of the early mining days in the Western fells was heightened by the lone prospectors who came to the district. They paid tribute to the owner of the fell in which they proposed to mine, then got to work on their own account; sometimes opening up a new vein, sometimes trying their luck with one which had been abandoned. One can imagine these lone wolves, hacking their own little entrance shaft, squeezing through the narrow fissure into the darkness and there working, day after day, with a lamp and solitude. Tales of rich strikes lured them on. If they found a good deposit of ore they kept the find strictly to themselves. Sometimes one would build up a hidden hoard, then die with his secret intact until another man unwittingly followed in his footsteps and stumbled over the hoard. Between the years of 1848 and 1865 two such stores of ore were discovered in the Barrow mine between Newlands and Braithwaite.

The Old Men, either as lone prospectors or in small groups, worked the old Brandley Mine (you will see their workings on the ridge of Catbells and for some distance below), the Barrow Mine and the Stoneycroft Mine, all well in the days before the use of gunpowder.

The Cromwellian destruction of the Keswick smelting-works did not, of course, spell the finish of mining in the district. The Dutch who came with Prince William of Orange began working Goldscope again; it is also thought they worked the Dale Head Mine. Smuggling of ore also began to thrive.

There is no record of Goldscope during the following century; it probably lay abandoned, as the Dutch believed it had been worked out. In 1847 it was reopened by a private company, who went bankrupt within eighteen months. Another private company then purchased the mine and also opened the old lead mine of Yewthwaite, in the junction between Catbells and Maiden Moor. This company struck it rich. Goldscope was abandoned in 1864 when the shaft had become so deep that the 40-foot wheel which pumped the water from it could no longer cope with the task. The mine was reopened yet again during the First World War, but has since been derelict. There are many people who can still recall this last working of Goldscope; one of my informants described how his grandfather had had the job of transporting the ore by horse-and-cart to Braithwaite Station. 'It was a hard pull for the horse.'

28 *Derwentwater, looking towards Causey Pike*

The history of Goldscope resembles that of all other mines in the District. Every mine in the Lake District, whether individually or company worked, has been basically a gamble, especially in the old days when mining methods were very primitive. A mine would be described as worked out, would change hands, be left derelict, then be opened again with excellent results. Valuable ores have even been found in old slag-heaps. There is no guarantee that some of these mines will not be reopened some time or the other and worked profitably once more.

The idea many Lakeland lovers nurse of a District always blissfully silent and deserted, where a few chosen spirits have wandered, cloud-lonely, absorbing untouched beauty and unbroken silence, is a misleading one; this in fact has always been an active, living land; a land that has belonged more truly to the busy Old Men clattering around their mines than to poetic and solitary wanderers.

Keswick, after the closing of the smelting-works, relapsed into a somewhat decayed state; it became a small, sleepy market-town again (it was Edward I who originally gave Keswick its charter for a market). A wool-trade and a pencil-making industry kept the town ticking quietly over, but a writer of 1749 described the place as 'much inferior to what it was formerly'.

Twenty years later Gray, the first tourist, arrived, to carry back such horrifying descriptions of Borrowdale and the back o' Skidda that no genuine lover of the romantically picturesque could wait to pack looking-glass and sketch-book and be away. Keswick in due course became a boom-town once more; a tourist boom, this time.

The only aspect of Borrowdale which may horrify you today is the rain. Borrowdale has the most famous rain in the world; the wettest, most living rain. Sometimes it simply drops solid, sometimes it swathes down the valley like tall grass before a scythe. Occasionally, in early spring, it comes down like steel knitting-needles, the air glittering with it, but in summer it is often plump, delicious, juicy rain like asparagus heads, so that you feel tempted to open your mouth to taste it. Here the rain always has a colour; grey, opaque, sleety-white, indigo, slate-green. In April I have seen pale blue rain falling upon a churchyard of daffodils, which sounds rather mawkish in print but was very beautiful to see.

177

It was in Borrowdale that I once stood in a shower talking to a friend who, a couple of yards further up the track, was in the dry; the rain stopped between us as if it were the end of a wall. Another time, going over Honister, the rain, falling some 15 yards ahead of me, travelled over the pass with me walking behind it like a shepherd after a flock of sheep; at the top of the pass the rain veered suddenly leftwards and whisked away over Brandreth. The rain here is so alive one is tempted to feel at times that it should have a vote.

Of course it is good local form to ignore the wet; which sometimes leads to extraordinary situations. For example, we once attended a sale in Borrowdale, held in a garden during an afternoon of solid downpour. The goods for auction were spread out in the garageway and a sizable crowd turned up, including the old ladies who always attend all the local sales; all in macs and sou'westers as though ready to man a life-boat. They sat themselves on the chairs provided and there they stayed, throughout the deluge. The rain rolled down our necks, trickled off our noses, stole inside our clothes, dripped on our boots. Yet not a solitary comment was made on the fact that it was raining; the whole thing passed off as though the afternoon were clear and dry.

And what is there for you to see in Borrowdale, apart from the celebrated rain (which with luck you might be spared)? Chiefly, I think, Borrowdale itself, unique in its juxtaposition of crag and foliage; rocks and birches cascading, intermingled, down the steep fellsides. In the dale bottom lie lush green intake-fields and the Derwent pursues an alternate course of foaming shallows and deep jade-coloured placidity.

Borrowdale has the Bowder Stone, a great lump of rock the size of a house, stranded like a petrified mammoth of the Ice Age. Then there are the Lodore Falls, best described by the tale of the man who asked where the falls were and was told he was sitting on them. There is the double-spanned pack-horse bridge at Grange and beyond Grange there is Castle Crag jutting sharply upwards just within the Jaws of Borrow-dale. You should try to go up Castle Crag; the pull up is steep but of short duration and the view from the top is wonderful. The crag was given to the National Trust in memory of Lieut. John Hamer and the men of Borrowdale who fell in the First World War.

The walk to the crag from Grange is lovely, while behind the crag lies a rocky little valley which you might explore. It was here that once (in the rain) I saw a fox creeping along the top of a wall, a wonderfully stealthy sight. At the time I was huddled under a bush, attempting to keep dry.

Walkers, serious ones, should remember that by following this track behind Castle Crag they reach Lobstone Band, an excellent way up to the *col* below Dale Head, from which they can do the marvellous Dale Head, Hindscarth, Robinson ridge-walk, one of the best the District has to offer.

By keeping along the track behind Castle Crag and then turning sharp left towards Borrowdale-bottom again, when you meet the beck that flows down from Lobstone Band, you can walk very pleasantly from Grange to Rosthwaite, keeping right off the main road. You should make time to stroll around Borrowdale just a little; bowling down it once in your car will reveal little of its finest beauty.

The District's last hermit, a man named Millican Dalton, lived in a cave on Castle Crag, just above the Derwent. As a child I several times saw him walking in the woods at the foot of Gate Crag, or crossing Grange Bridge. I used to think that it would be wonderful to be a hermit here. Indeed, your first glimpse of Borrowdale may seduce you into wondering if you might not try becoming a hermit here yourself; practical reasons will doubtless persuade you against it, but it is an attractive notion.

A wonderful place to stroll up is the Lang Strath valley, which you reach through the hamlet of Stonethwaite, lying beyond the central village of Rosthwaite. Since the Lang Strath has two bridges you can walk up one side of the valley and return along the other. At the head of the valley rises Bowfell and by climbing straight up and out of the valley bottom you would arrive on Esk Hause, close to Angle Tarn and that Shelter which is no shelter.

On the left of the Lang Strath head ascends the Stake Pass, taking you over to the Langdales. Borrowdale is the valley which, all in all, penetrates most deeply into the heart of the District.

Borrowdale has always been a deep, enclosed place and the people who lived here in earlier times earned a name for being so much out of this world that they were nicknamed *gowks*, which is the local name both for a cuckoo and a dimwit; there is that old song about the cuckoo being a silly bird. The nickname of the Borrowdale folk is given edge by the fact that local legend says that they were the people who tried to preserve eternal spring by walling the cuckoo into their valley. Personally I can never understand why the cuckoo is regarded as silly; it seems to me to be just the reverse, seeing that it has neatly solved the problem of how to get its offspring raised wholly by the exertions of others. Similarly one feels that the alleged dimness of the Borrowdale folk lay not in themselves, but in the perception of those who viewed them from outside. Something of the old attitude still persists among visitors and the essence of Borrowdale is summed up, I think, in this conversation, reported two or three summers back in the *Keswick Reminder*:

> Lady visitor, enthusing to Borrowdale native whom she has discovered sunning himself on a stone: Isn't this a lovely, lovely spot?
> Native: Aye, it is.
> Visitor: Yes, it really is enchanting. . . . All the same, I simply couldn't live here all the year round . . . there's nothing to do!
> Native: That's why I live here.

The Norse colonised this valley in the tenth and eleventh centuries; they called it Bogardalr, which in Icelandic means the 'dale of the Borg', the *borg* in this instance being in all probability Castle Crag. Watendlath, the tiny cluster of farms lying by a tarn high and secluded in the fell between Borrowdale and Thirlmere, was one of their *saeters* and you can now reach it either on foot from Rosthwaite, up a stony but delightful track, or by car along the narrow road behind Barrow House, spoilt now in the season by the number of people taking the drive, but still a route of great beauty in autumn or winter, perhaps especially winter. Ashness Bridge, seen in snow, is lovelier than it ever is in August. There is another fine pack-pony bridge at Watendlath itself.

The Furness monks farmed at Borrowdale, most of which, by 1209, they owned. After the Dissolution came a period of some 60 years during which the history of Borrowdale went unrecorded; in 1613 two typical Tudor tycoons, Messrs Whitmore and Verdon, shrewd land-agents, purchased whole areas of Borrowdale which they in turn sold at a profit to private individuals, including Sir Wilfred Lawson,

and a Lamplugh, to mention two names to become famous in the District. Watendlath, which had belonged to Fountains, not Furness, became the seat of a small wool-spinning industry.

When Gray came as a tourist to Borrowdale, avoiding going too far up the valley because of its dangers, the eagles still nested on their crag which lies on the left of the entrance to the Lang Strath. They caused great havoc amongst the sheep, so that the shepherds 'lost abundance of lambs yearly', reported Gray. One eyrie in the breeding-season was said to have accounted for one lamb a day, besides wild vermin caught and consumed. It is no small wonder that the shepherds annually plundered the nest. The birds finally despaired of raising a brood in Borrowdale and departed, it is said, to Eskdale, in 1786, where the male bird was killed. Most of the wilder dales had had eagles and in every dale the shepherds had waged war against the birds, so that their disappearance from the District by the end of the nineteenth century was only to be expected, indeed it was intended. However, of recent years golden eagles have been authentically sighted over the Lakes and ornithologists are talking, hopefully, of perhaps one day having eagles nesting in Lakeland again. This would raise a difficult problem for the shepherds, since the eagles would no doubt be protected birds. It is perhaps to be hoped that they will not try to return to their former haunts.

There are five villages in Borrowdale; Grange, Rosthwaite, Stonethwaite, Seathwaite and Seatoller, although strictly speaking they are hamlets rather than villages. The way to the Sty lies through Seathwaite; the pass rises beyond Stockley Bridge. You cannot drive beyond Seathwaite and anyway there is little to see unless you are going to walk.

Near Seathwaite, on the other side of the beck (the infant Derwent), was the famous wadd-mine which I have already mentioned in connection with the mystery of Moses. This wadd, or plumbago, mine was already famous in the time of Elizabeth I and the pencil industry had already started in Keswick. It is thought that the mine was first worked by the Furness monks. After the Dissolution the Crown got possession of it. Later it came into the hands of the Lawson family and in 1662 it passed into ownership of the Bankes. The plumbago, or wadd, was of great value, especially after it began to be used for munition-making. The mine was the most important of its kind in Europe; indeed it was

183

thought to be the only mine of high-grade wadd in the world. Naturally a great deal of smuggling of the precious substance went on; during the reign of George II a special Act of Parliament was passed for its protection. The miners were stripped and searched on leaving their work to make sure they had not stolen any wadd, a building was erected over the principal level's entry and armed men were kept on guard there during the night. When the graphite was sent to the Company's warehouse in London an armed escort accompanied it as far as Kendal. Nevertheless, despite these precautions, smuggling went on; it is said that illicit purchasers came regularly to the George Hotel, Keswick, to buy it. How it got to the George Hotel is anybody's guess.

The mine-tips were regularly searched by thieves; the tale goes that if one went near the mine, some nights, one saw dozens of lanterns twinkling and moving over the tips.

A famous deposit of wadd discovered in the mine in 1803 yielded $31\frac{3}{4}$ tons, totally valued at about £100,000.

There are stirring tales of battles between guards and smugglers; I possess an old engraving of a gunfight going on beneath Honister Crag: armed horsemen are pouring up from the direction of Buttermere, while ferocious-looking types fire on them from the lower slopes of Dalehead. What it is really all about there is no saying, but one feels that it is in all probability something to do with smugglers and wadd. In view of the theory that Moses was a wadd-smuggling Honister quarryman this picture is, I think, particularly interesting.

The plumbago mine (wadd, graphite, plumbago are all three names for the same substance) finally became uneconomic and closed. The Cumberland Pencil Company still flourishes in Keswick, but it is many years now since the pencils were made with Seathwaite graphite. The new pencil factory stands to the east of the Greta as you enter Keswick from the Crosthwaite church direction; westwards of the new factory, close by the Greta-side, is the old factory and a very interesting showroom where you can see exhibits of plumbago and so forth from the old mine.

Seathwaite is notorious as the wettest place in the country. This, as Lakeland supporters earnestly tell you, doesn't mean that it rains more often here than elsewhere, it means that when it rains it does so *harder*. Quality, rather than quantity, as it were.

There are six rain gauges; one at the farm at Seathwaite itself, one at Stockley Bridge, one at Sty Head Tarn, two at Styhead and one at Sprinkling Tarn. On the first day of each month they are read and the readings recorded by Mr Edmondson of the farm. The figures are sent to the Meteorological Office at Harrow. The task of a long and rugged walk, monthly, in all weathers, round the rain gauges demands, one feels, a born connoisseur of high-grade rain. But in time everyone in Borrowdale tends to become expert on the subject of downpours. One finds oneself automatically turning into a cloud-watcher if one spends much time in the Lake District; just as in dryer counties one is attracted to bird-watching. I am a keen cloud-watcher, although unable to decide what is my favourite species of cloud. I think, perhaps, those great, slow, detached ones which come swimming, like white whales, down the higher valleys when the weather is changing warm and fair; these clouds pass slowly, one by one, either in schools or at intervals, on a level with the house so that one can sit watching them as they go, perhaps two hundred yards or so distant, ponderous and serene, as one imagines Moby Dick to have travelled when Captain Ahab wasn't on his tail.

Robinson provides, I think, the best vantage-point for cloud-watching; from some sheltered ledge on his northern face you get terrific views on wild days of the long processions of clouds that travel the Grasmoor, Wandope, Causey Pike ridge. Then, abruptly, you yourself become engulfed in cloud, steaming up from below, or pouring down on you from a gully. For a moment you are quite shut away from the world; there you sit, encased in soundless white vapour, until the cloud-fabric splits and through the widening rents you can see Wandope and Causey Pike again with the cloud cohorts still marching over them.

Below Robinson's lower western plateau of Buttermere Moss lies the little village of Buttermere, the lake after which the village takes its name, the lazy Dubs connecting Buttermere with Crummock Water (a dub is a pool in a river). To see these two beautiful lakes one should drive from Keswick over the Whinlatter Pass, then drive from Lorton towards Scalehill and thus up the eastern shore of Crummock Water; in this way you travel into the dalehead; for the best views of a dale it should always be travelled into. Crummock, twice as long as Buttermere, has a very special beauty of shoreline and is graced at its head with several small islands. Together with Buttermere and Lowes Water it once formed one long glacial lake. Buttermere, when you gain it beyond the village, is peacock-blue, emerald-green and indigo; on its western shore stand Red Pike, High Stile and High Crag, with Sour Milk Ghyll falling down the fellside below Red Pike, a dash of white water from dark Bleaberry Tarn tucked in the hanging-valley under the Pike. Between High Stile and High Crag is Birkness Combe, a great place for ravens and rock-climbers. I can still see my sister, always blithe, even when risking her neck on a rope with me, scattering fragments of crust around her, and when I asked her what on earth she was doing she made the gay reply, 'Oh, just putting out a little bread for the ravens.' 'Quite the Elijah, aren't you? Heavens, do you imagine they eat *bread*?' 'Why not? They will probably welcome a change of diet. I can't suppose that many people come up here and put out bread for them.' Recalling the place on which she was perched as she spoke, I cannot suppose that many did either.

If you stay in Buttermere you will find many heavenly walks, some mild, some middling and some strenuous. This is the scene of some of my happiest childhood holidays, so I could trot you around very pleasantly not forgetting to take you on Haystacks, at the head of Buttermere, or exploring the corrie of Warnscale Bottom, or following the ridge-walk of Red Pike, High Stile and High Crag, with Ennerdale and the Pillar to thrill you on your right and the Robinson, Hindscarth, Dalehead ridge on your left across Buttermere. I would take you up Ruddy Beck to Ling Combe, or into Rannerdale, we would go up Grasmoor, we would go to Scale Force; all over the place in fact so that you wouldn't have any legs left.

Scale Force is the most impressive waterfall in the District. This, I grant, means little, but Scale Force with its 125-foot drop, deep in a rocky cleft, is quite spectacular, especially after heavy rain. You have to climb up a slippery ladder to see it properly, and walk along a very muddy track to reach the slippery ladder, so your trip will be rather more strenuous, anyway, than if you visit Niagara. This may make it memorable for you. Coleridge and George Eliot both visited Scale Force in their day, amongst other notables; the track was better kept then than it is now, you can still see the remains of a granite causeway here and there, but nowadays the way to Scale Force is peaty and wet and you will need very sensible shoes. From Buttermere village Scale Force is a distance of two miles; you cannot take a car any nearer to the Force than the village. If you prefer it you may hire a boat and row to Ling Crag, leaving the lethargic on the shingle-ridge there to guard boat and picnic things while you trudge up-country (about three-quarters of-a-mile) to look at the Force.

Before leaving Buttermere you should visit the tiny church, where, long ago, the vicar always preached a certain sermon for each certain Sunday of the year and so we always got the Queen of Sheba going to visit Solomon. Another sermon concerned the ark of the Lord in the field and on one occasion, when the good man preached at Lorton and lingered somewhat over the ark, a Lorton parishioner, visiting Buttermere a week or so later, enquired if, 'Buttermere parson had got t'ark out o' t' field yet?'

The drive back to Keswick should be by Honister Pass, under Honister Crag and past the slate-quarries. The other side of the pass takes you down to Seatoller; you are back in Borrowdale.

Before you finally leave this part of the District you should climb Catbells. Maybe you didn't get up Scafell Pike, or Great Gable, or any of the other walks I have suggested, but do please try Catbells. We once got a friend up there whose sole comment to any suggestion of walking was that of Eliza Doolittle, 'Not bloody likely'. But we did finally get him up Catbells; true we carried up gin and vermouth to lure him up the final pitch, but even without promise of such a finishing touch to your exertions I am sure that you will never regret the effort. From the top (which gives a sensation of being much higher than it actually is) you will look down on Derwentwater with its islands and boats, on Keswick with its Gothic-steepled St John's, old Crosthwaite lying distant on the left, under Skiddaw. You will see Saddleback, and Borrowdale enclosed from view by the famous Jaws. On your left lies Newlands, with Causey Pike, Robinson, Hindscarth and Dalehead. Now you can see at a glance how close these valleys are, how fraternal the fells with one another, how fraternal the clouds with the fells. You may hear the 'cronk cronk' of the two ravens who live on a neighbouring spur, or see the old buzzard wheeling high over Littletown, while rain skirmishes over the long waters of Bassenthwaite. You will be glad that you climbed up here.

CHAPTER TEN

Ullswater and Mardale

'Ullswater', says Ackermann, 'is the noblest of the English lakes.' This is both true and untrue. Ullswater has three reaches; the lower is set in flattish, drowsy surroundings, pretty but placid like the steamers which ply at the pier and the cows which browse in the meadows. The scenery of the centre-basin is altogether more picturesque, as Baddeley says; here is Howtown with the Fusedale Beck behind it and the long High Street range overshadowing everything. The third reach, or basin, is a marvellous expanse of water, entered between Glencoyne Park on the one hand and Silver Point on the other. St Sunday Crag commands the head of the lake, with Place Fell on the left and Stybarrow Crag on the right. The water is ever-changing with sheens of light and reflections. Lovely at all times of the year, Ullswater's head is most beautiful in early spring when there is snow still on the tops and the trees of the shore are etched in clear outline against the silver of the lake.

Ullswater was famous with the Romantic tourists for its echoes. To quote Ackermann again: 'Cannon are kept at the inn, for the gratification of travellers, the effect of the discharge of which is very appalling. . . .' At Pooley Bridge the Earl of Surrey had formerly kept a barge for eight rowers, mounting twelve swivel-guns for the purpose of rousing the echoes, and any visitor could enjoy the facilities of this barge for a small fee. One can imagine the reactions of the Friends of the Lake District if some enterprising capitalist tried to revive this attraction on Ullswater today.

After reading of all this raising of echoes one is not surprised to learn that the great numbers of wild ducks which once had bred on Ullswater had removed themselves elsewhere.

For persons who come to this part of the world to walk, pretty little Sandwick, on the eastern shore of Ullswater a mile-and-a-half above Howtown, provides a very good base. From it may be explored Boardale and Bannerdale, Martindale, High Street, Ramsghyll and Kidsty Pike and the fells round Angle Tarn (not to be confused with the Esk Hause Angle Tarn). This, once again, is all country my father taught me. Even today the High Street Range, Kidsty, Caudale Moor, Ill Bell, Harter Fell and Bampton Common provide marvellously unspoilt territory. Here, if you go quietly, you may well sight red deer, or wild fell ponies.

Deer have been greatly on the increase in the District during the past decade, indeed their rapid spread in numbers has been causing concern. The red deer thrive on the Helvellyn range, in the plantations of Thirlmere and in the Martindale Forest, this last having been a deer forest since the time of Elizabeth I. Lately the red deer have been infiltrating through Westmorland down to the Lune valley. The roe deer too are on the increase, appearing recently in many places where they have not been seen before. A population-burst among the deer could well present serious problems, for deer do more damage amongst young plantations and crops than is generally realised. The severe winter of 1963 is said, however, to have considerably depleted the numbers of deer.

The fell ponies, some of which still roam wild over High Street, are native to the fells of Cumberland and Westmorland. They are dark, quite sizable and rugged-looking. In winter their coats become immensely thick. In former days they were used as pack-ponies and they are now becoming increasingly popular as a children's pony. I have often thought it would be a useful notion to keep a fell pony for jogging about on in the dales and over the lower fell-sides; I might possibly explore this notion further as an old woman? 'Here comes that eccentric old soul on her pony. . . .' Maybe.

There is a flourishing Fell Pony Society which welcomes enquiries from those interested in these very delightful animals.

Beatrix Potter once saw four wild fell ponies on Troutbeck Tongue encircling a tree with measured canter; round and round, then checking and turning, like ponies trained for public performance, dancing ponies.

Foxes, of course, are common in the District, in some seasons they are rife. More will be written of them presently. Badgers too are common, though but rarely seen by the ordinary walker. The rabbits have almost disappeared; one hears conflicting accounts of the increase of mountain-hares. The red squirrels are one of the District's greatest delights. Pine-martens, once common, became very rare indeed; some people claimed extinction for them, but an informant who is deeply knowledgeable on these things but likes to keep his knowledge private tells me that they are becoming comfortably re-established in some of the high forestry plantations. The pole-cat, or foumart, is extinct. One of the advantages and pleasures of being a solitary, and therefore a silent, walker is that one sees so much more of wild-life on the fells than do those who always walk in company.

People always ask when it was that wolves disappeared from the District. Packs of wolf-hounds were kept in these parts until as late as the reign of Charles II, but that does not necessarily mean that there were wolves to hunt. It is thought that the last wolf was killed in the District in the fifteenth century by Sir John Harrington at Humphrey Head in Morecambe Bay. Other sources say that there were wolves in the centre-fells at least a century later than this. My sister and I used to believe (had we read it somewhere?) that their final retreat had been the Glaramara caves; I remember an expedition to the caves which ended in panic because lively imagination convinced us that at any moment we might meet with a wolf.

Wild boar were also a great feature of the District's wild-life in the Middle-ages, while the Romans hunted brown bears too. The District can offer nothing more alarming these days than its cows, of which it produces a savage breed. I am not particularly scared of cows, ordinary cows. I am not like darling Dorothy Wordsworth, who tells us in her Journal how: 'I went through the fields, and sate $\frac{1}{2}$ an hour afraid to pass a cow. The cow looked at me, and I looked at the cow, and whenever I stirred the cow gave over eating.' But I do greatly dislike these young animals one so frequently encounters in the higher dales; I am sure it is only high spirits and curiosity which fetches them running, but their manner *is* aggressive and they show an inordinate desire to bump one from behind. Only the other evening a friend and I had a most unpleasant experience of being chased by a herd of young cows while searching for the Duke of Somerset's old smelting-furnaces in

Dale Head. The mad scene which took place, with myself and companion facing the enemy with all the determination and frenzy of Custer's Last Stand, is best left to the imagination. I was carrying a small oil lamp with which I had been examining the rock-surface of the mouth of one of the old mines (this sounds ridiculous, but I could not find an electric torch) and I advanced upon the cows waving this oil-lamp at them, like a demented Florence Nightingale. So far as I am concerned the District needs no wolves or boars while there are cows around.

But how much worse when Mrs Lynn Linton was writing! 'Bulls cannot be kept sane in these narrow valleys: the constantly repeated echoes of their own bellowing make them mad', she tells us. There is 'always a mad bull somewhere in the lake district; and awful brutes they are to look at, and something more than awful to meet.' She then goes on to tell us about the famous mad 'man-keen' bull of Seathwaite in Borrowdale which apparently used to be kept in the intake-fields by the beck. 'This mad bull of Seathwaite had a no mean list of killed and damaged, more or less true, tacked to its reputation; and, indeed, even a brave man might own to something like tremor at the sight of its fierce head thrust above a low stone wall, its eyes literally flashing with fiery red rage, foam hanging about its lips and nostrils . . . its voice a low, harsh grunt. . . . The wall looked perilously low, and the padlocked gate seemed dangerously old and crazy, when we passed the field where our "man-keen" friend was snorting and grunting. . . .'[1]

Mrs Linton should have known what she was talking about; she was born and bred in the District, but this seems to have been a terrible animal indeed.

Let us hasten back to the fells round Ullswater and take a look at Martindale, lying well below Angle Tarn, between Boardale and Bannerdale. Martindale has two churches, a modern one down the dale at Cowgarth and an old one further up the dale, on the bank of Howe Grain, near the hamlet under Wintercrag. There has been a church in Martindale on this Howe Grain site since the early thirteenth century, although this actual building was erected on the site of the former church in 1633. The interior is fascinating, with good seventeenth-century woodwork. Here we encounter the shade of one of those

[1] E. Lynn Linton, *The Lake Country*.

incredibly thrifty clergymen the District seems to have specialised in; one Richard Birkett, who was parson here for 67 years, on a stipend of £20 a year. He brought up a family and died worth £1,200. The truth, according to Clarke, was that the old parson 'being except one the only man in the parish who could write . . . transacted most of the law affairs of his parishioners. Whenever he lent money, he deducted at the time of lending two shillings in the pound for interest, and the term of the loan never exceeded a year; he charged for writing a receipt two-pence, and for a promissory note, four pence; and used such other acts of extortion as one would scarce believe to have been practised in so contracted a sphere. He likewise taught a school, and served as parish-clerk; and in both these offices he likewise shewed his wonderful turn for economy and gain; for his quarter's dues from his scholars being small, he had from the parents of each scholar, a fort-night's board and lodging; and the Easter dues being usually paid in eggs, he, at the time of collecting, carried with him a board in which was a hole, which served him as a gauge, and he positively refused to accept any which would pass through.' Furthermore 'he married a woman named Brown, with whom he got a fortune of 60l'.[1]

If you are seriously walking we will leave you to explore your high and lonely fells while we take a look at some of the attractions of the lake shores. Of these Aira Force should be mentioned; the track to the force starts at the point where the Dockray and Troutbeck road leaves the lakeside. The force itself is, like all the District's waterfalls, only impressive after heavy rain, but the surroundings are very pretty; Ackermann declares them 'highly fascinating'. Nearby is Lyulph's Tower, a great favourite with romantics. The tower is an eighteenth-century shooting-box, but it supposedly stands on the site of an earlier one built by Lyulph, first Baron of Greystoke, whose name is said to derive from an ancestor, Ulf; from this source might also come the name of Ullswater.

Gowbarrow Park is where Dorothy Wordsworth saw the daffodils when she was out walking with William on April 15th 1802.

For those who are interested in the District's ancient history the lower reach of Ullswater may possibly prove more exciting than the upper, beautiful as these upper reaches are. Dunmallet, a low wooded

[1] Clarke, *Survey of the Lakes*.

hill to the west of Pooley Bridge, is the site of a British hill-fort while nearby at Caerthanock is another British fort. At Eamont Bridge, just before you reach Penrith, are two mound-encircled rings, one on the right and one on the left of the road respectively, their names Mayborough and King Arthur's Round Table: many explanations are given for their origin. Certainly King Arthur's Round Table was once used as an amphitheatre for local sports; cock-fighting, bull-baiting and the like, but it goes back much further than this in time. The Mayborough earthwork is on slightly raised ground and until the eighteenth century great stones stood there, but the local people decided to cart them away and used them for domestic building purposes so that now only one stone remains.

Moor Divock is another place where archaeologists (and fell-walkers too) may wander with profit and pleasure: this expanse of fell lies between Pooley Bridge and Bampton and is a good lonely place to walk over. Its particular interest lies in the many prehistoric sites to be discovered. The Victorian archaeologist-doctor of Penrith, Dr Michael W. Taylor, thought that he had found traces of stone alignments but Professor Collingwood, another Moor Divock enthusiast, said that for his part he was never able to distinguish these.

Criminologists can rouse themselves here: Dr Taylor was the brother of Mary Jane Pritchard, second murder victim and wife of Dr Edward William Pritchard, the notorious Glasgow poisoner (his first victim was old Mrs Taylor, his mother-in-law). Devotees of Dr Pritchard will remember that the Taylor family wished the mysteriously ailing Mary Jane to go to her brother at Penrith for a while to see if the change of air would do her good, but Dr Pritchard refused to fall in with the suggestion.

So, having wandered around the ancient sites of the lower reach of Ullswater, having visited the western shore's Aira Force, Lyulph's Tower and Gowbarrow Park of the central reach, or, if you walk, having made either Howtown or Sandwick a base for some of the finest days on the fells obtainable throughout the entire District, the time has now come to move to the head of the lake. Walkers will take the track along the eastern shoreline, past Silver Hill and Bleawick, under Place Fell. By the western shore the motor-road skirts Glencoyne Park, passes Glenridding and Patterdale Hall and thence into Patterdale itself.

Patterdale church is dedicated to St Patrick and nearby is St Patrick's Well, but modern opinion holds that St Patrick never came near this dale, in spite of its name. The foundation of the church is Elizabethan, though the building we see is a fairly modern one. Old yews in the churchyard, a seventeenth-century Bible and plate and a font, the stem of which is thirteenth-century, speak of a long past and although the experts today are firm in the view that St Patrick never set foot in these dales there is no guarantee that new information will not be forthcoming at some future date to establish exactly the reverse.

Patterdale too rejoiced in a miraculously thrifty parson, the early and mid-eighteenth-century Mattison, minister of Patterdale for 60 years (he lived to be 90). During the early part of his life his stipend was £12 a year; later it was increased to £18 a year, which it never exceeded. Mattison, we are told, married on this income, brought up four children, educating one son at college, lived at a reasonable standard of comfort and left over £1,000 when he died. What subterfuges *he* indulged in I have been unable to discover. It may have been the Mattisons that Dorothy heard about from her friends the Clarksons, who lived near Ullswater. Says Dorothy in her Journal: 'Mrs Clarkson knew a clergyman and his wife who brought up ten children upon a curacy, sent two sons to college, and he left £1,000 when he died. The wife was very generous, gave to all poor people victuals and drink. She had a passion for feeding animals. She killed a pig with feeding it over much. When it was dead she said, "To be sure, it's a great loss, but I thank God it did not die *clemmed*" (the Cheshire word for starved). . . .'

About a quarter of a mile from the church is seventeenth-century Patterdale Hall, extensively rebuilt now, but with a doorway marked I. and D.M. 1677; the house was known then as the Palace of Patterdale, for it was here lived the Mounseys, 'kings' of Patterdale. These remote dales were frequently presided over by one particular family which claimed sovereignty; for example, the famous Holme dynasty of Mardale. The Patterdale Mounseys traced their dale supremacy back to the day when an ancestor had led his fellow dalesmen into battle against a band of marauding Scots (who, I suppose, came over the Sticks Pass). The Mounsey Dynasty lasted until 1824 when a family named Marshall came to Patterdale Hall.

Here is Dorothy's Journal for December 21st 1801, giving us some

fascinating contemporary gossip about the Mounseys of that day:
'When we were at Thomas Ashburner's on Sunday Peggy talked about
the Queen of Patterdale. She had been brought to drinking by her
husband's unkindness and avarice. She was formerly a very nice tidy
woman. She had taken to drinking but that was better than if she had
taken to something worse (by this I suppose she meant killing herself).
She said that her husband used to be out all night with other women
and she used to *hear* him come in in the morning, for they never slept
together—"Many a poor body, a wife like me, has had a working heart
for her, as much stuff as she had." . . .'

Sticks Pass, the presumed route of the invading Scots whom the
Patterdale men repulsed, is the old pack-pony route between Thirlmere
and the Greenside Lead Mines. The highest part of the pass is marked by
sticks stuck into the ground at intervals instead of the more usual
cairns; this stick method of route-marking dates back to the monks.
The Pass touches the edge of the old reservoir (which was created for
mining purposes) while below the reservoir is the famous Greenside
Lead Mine itself.

This mine, Postlethwaite tells us, was first opened in the latter part
of the eighteenth century, but was not worked extensively until about
the year 1825. Before that time the mine had been worked chiefly near
the surface, the ore being carried over the Sticks Pass to the smelt-
works at Stoneycroft Ghyll in Newlands. From 1825 onwards the mine
was worked at an ever increasing profit; the mine at all stages having
been highly mechanised according to the standards of the day.

The principal ore of this mine was galena, producing, when smelted,
about 80 per cent of lead and 12 ounces of silver per ton. In the later
years of the mine the ore was smelted at the mine itself and the silver
extracted from it; for this a chimney was carried up the side of the
mountain for a distance of one and a half miles, in order that the lead
which flew off in vapour from the furnaces might better condense. This
chimney had man-holes at intervals, so that it might be periodically
swept. Many a fell-walker has been puzzled by the chimney.

It was not until recently that the Greenside Mine closed; the miners'
huts are now used as a Youth Hostel.

There is an interesting little walk back from the mine; across a
footbridge by the mill, then down a track which runs beside the beck

to join a larger path at Gillside. You can then either follow this track into Glenridding, or traverse the breast of fell between yourself and Grisedale, thereby obtaining a very beautiful view down the lake. Dropping down the side of the breast you will then connect with the Grassthwaitehow track, which will lead you down to Patterdale.

But the great walking expedition of this area is, of course, the ascent of Helvellyn. Although Helvellyn may be climbed from Thirlmere, from Wythburn, from Grasmere by Dollywaggon Pike, and many ways more, the ascent from Patterdale, although the longest, is the best, going up by the Keppelcove Pony-track (as it is marked on the map), then following the ridge over Low Man and thus arriving at the summit and the so-called shelter above Red Tarn.

Red Tarn lies deep in a magnificent horse-shoe, the two curving arms of which are Swirrel Edge terminating in Catchedicam, and the notorious Striding Edge. Swirrel is another form of Swirl, but Catchedicam is a name that takes some analysing. It breaks down thus: *cat*, a cat, *sty*, a way or a pass, or in this case a ladder, *cam*, the crest of a hill. So the old name, Catstyecam (which over the long years has turned into Catchedicam), means the top of the cat's ladder; a highly descriptive name for the place as no doubt you will agree when you have reached it.

Striding Edge looks fearful in photographs but in reality is perfectly safe (except in icy conditions) and not at all frightening for anyone with my usually stipulated sound head and steady feet. There is only one part which tends to be nasty and that is the final lap, from the summit on to the ridge, but even this part of the route is perfectly safe if approached with reasonable care.

No doubt many people automatically think of Helvellyn as a dangerous mountain because they are always carrying at the back of their minds the story of Gough and his dog. Although Helvellyn's most celebrated fatal accident took place as long ago as 1805 the story of the faithful dog who kept watch over the body of her master after he had fallen to his death still appeals strongly to the imagination. You will see the memorial Canon Rawnsley erected at the site of the accident in memory of the dog's moving three months' vigil.

Many visitors, reaching the head of Ullswater and having seen what they wanted to see and climbed what they wanted to climb, will leave by the Kirkstone Pass. We have already glimpsed it from the Troutbeck side, that part of the Pass known as 'the Struggle'; we must now visualise ourselves approaching from the Patterdale side.

There are three good valleys at the head of Ullswater which a walker will be interested in, rather than start plodding over the traffic-worried Kirkstone. Therefore let us pause for a moment, reader, before you start your drive up the Pass and note these valleys for the benefit of those who do not wish to drive. They are Grisedale, with its foot-pass, Deepdale and Dovedale. These two last are well worth a pedestrian's attention.

The main-road skirts Brothers Water, once known as Broad Water but later renamed after two brothers said to have been drowned there. To your left lies Low Hartsop, an attractive little village to which we walkers will return in a moment when we have shown the motorist the Pass. A little beyond Brothers Water to the right is Hartsop Hall, dating to the sixteenth century and now a farm, but formerly the home of the de Lancasters, then of Sir John Lowther who became the first Lord Lonsdale at the end of the seventeenth century. In the eighteenth century the Hall had an extension built on to it which absorbed part of an ancient bridle-path right-of-way; the right-of-way now ran through the house and at least one dalesman, for many years, made a point of using this right-of-way at regular, if somewhat ceremonial, intervals. The right-of-way through the house still exists.

And now starts the long pull up the Pass, still a desolate place in spite of the traffic which flows over it. Ackermann, describing the Pass, observed that, 'On the sides of the mountain are immense peat mosses where, in the summer season, may be seen small parties of women and children digging and preparing the turf, which in several parts forms the only fuel of the inhabitants. In this occupation, which falls exclusively to the female part of the family, the wives of the dalesmen, of four, five and six hundred a year, may be seen labouring with their maids.'

These days no women, no mistresses and their maids and children, are to be seen cutting turf in the peat mosses. Nothing of any special note is to be seen, in fact, save the long, winding road. According to Baddeley the rock from which the Pass is named, the Kirkstone, lies to the right of the road, a little short of the top on this, the Patterdale, side, but there are so many boulders hereabouts and none looks particularly like a church.

The Kirkstone Pass Inn is able to boast of being the sixth highest licensed premises in the country, at 1,468 feet above sea-level. It is believed to have been built in 1840; certainly Ackermann (published in 1821) made no mention of any inn at the summit of the Pass. It is thought that Parson Sewell of Troutbeck may have had it built, for the refreshment of travellers, including himself.

Sewell was vicar of Troutbeck for 40 years, dying in 1869 at the age of 88. He was headmaster of Kelsick School, Ambleside, for 58 years. He was a man of pithy commonsense, likely to build an inn where one was much needed. My favourite Sewell story is of the time when a parishioner asked him to pray for rain, to receive the reply, 'It's no use praying for rain while t'wind's in this quarter'.

The Kirkstone Inn has been much modernised in recent years and now bears no resemblance to what it was in former times. It used to be a great place for shepherds' meets and merry neets and here too the fox-hunters would relax at the end of a run. It has seen lively nights.

And now, reader, if you are motoring I don't know quite what to suggest that you should do; our common goal is Mardale, but unless you retrace your tracks to Pooley Bridge you will now have to drive down the further side of the Pass, to Windermere, from Windermere go to Kendal, from Kendal cross the Shap fells to Shap itself and here turn left for Bampton and Hawes Water. This would probably be just as quick as going round the other way. I will leave you to work out your route while I return to the walkers we left at Brothers Water, casting an eye at Low Hartsop.

This, as I said, is a pretty village with some very attractive old buildings. This way too lies the pedestrian track by Hayes Water to Hawes Water and Mardale, starting by way of Hayeswater Ghyll. Hayes Water is a large and lonely tarn which your track does not in fact quite touch, but it is worth deviating from the route a little to see the tarn. Then back to your way over the Knott and Kidsty Pike and so down to Hawes Water. Here, as usual, the pedestrian will be able to enjoy himself better than the motorist.

I suppose everyone knows the story of Mardale; how Hawes Water was turned into a Manchester Corporation Reservoir, the Water's

32 *Striding Edge, Helvellyn, from Nethermost Pike*

volume being so greatly increased that the better part of Mardale vanished, drowned. The mediæval church, the hamlet of Mardale Green, the seventeenth-century Old Dun Bull Inn (place of so many shepherds' meets and merry neets, so many sports gatherings and hunts, where so many toasts had been drunk and so many celebrative tatie-pots had been eaten), the farms, Measand Hall, ancient home of the Bland family, Measand School, founded in 1711, all drowned. Thus came to the end an entire (though admittedly very small) community with a history dating back a thousand years and more. Of course it was all very efficiently done, with consideration. A new Dun Bull was built, a fine new road was constructed along the eastern side of the immensely swollen Hawes Water. But these things could not mitigate the dam, 1,550 feet in length, with a maximum height of 120 feet, the level of the lake now 90 feet higher than it was in nature. The living heart of Mardale had stopped beating when the waters closed overhead.

Still, Mardale is yet a very beautiful place.

This, in the old days, was the kingdom of the Holme family. Hugh Holme, the first of these kings of Mardale, fled north to Mardale in 1209 after having been involved in a plot against King John. Holme took refuge in a cave in Riggindale, tucked under Kidsty Pike, in a cave still known as Hugh's Cave. Then, after the death of King John, he emerged from Riggindale, but remained in Mardale, marrying to found the long dynasty of Holme 'kings of Mardale' which lasted without a break until 1885, with the death of the last male in the direct line, another, and final, Hugh Holme; providentially, perhaps, for it would have been a terrible thing for a Holme to have lived to see Mardale drown in 1940.

There are the remains of a prehistoric fort on Castle Crag at the head of Mardale, while Elizabethan Thornthwaite Hall still survives at the lower end of the Water. This Hall belonged to the Curwen family, from the time of the Conquest until when, in the seventeenth century, it was sold to the Howards. However, as I have said, it is the pedestrian who will see most round and about Mardale, for there is some wonderful walking here, including the exploration of Mardale Common and Swindale, the route taken until 1729 by the Mardale dead, strapped to the backs of ponies for conveyance to Shap for burial.

The road ends at the head of Hawes Water, only the pedestrian then

33 *Wrestling at Grasmere Sports*

can take one or other of the two tracks: leftwards for Gatescarth and Long Sleddale, to the right for Nan Bield and Kentmere.

Towards Nan Bield Pass we will look, for here comes a most remarkable procession, headed by an over-dressed woman of uncertain age, berouged and possibly bewigged, wearing a splendid feathered bonnet secured by a rather tatty scarf tied under the chin, wrapped in a large black cloak which looks as if it belonged to Hamlet, under the cloak a riding-habit green and shiny with age and wear, and on her feet hussar-style boots. She looks as if she had dressed from out of a property-box. A glance at the procession behind her, more ponies, some of them ridden by other ladies, younger than herself, but equally oddly dressed, several men of actor-like demeanour, yes, unmistakably so, one or two of them mounted, the others on foot and complaining mightily, ponies laden with boxes and bundles, some of the bundles very badly wrapped and fastened so that we glimpse vivid costumes and worn velvet curtains, more men, driving the ponies or carrying loads, and an enormously stout woman riding a little donkey, on each of her fat arms a wicker-hamper, convinces us that we must be looking at some kind of a charade. Almost we are right in our guess, but not exactly so. In fact we are seeing the arrival in Mardale of the famous Mrs Deans, together with her touring theatrical company. Kendal has been hit by cholera, the roads through the town have to be avoided, and so Mrs Deans has brought her company over the Nan Bield Pass, complete with costumes and baggage, grease-paints and props. They are booked to appear at Mardale and after Mardale at Bampton: the shows must go on.

Mrs Deans's exact age cannot be given; she was born at Wigton and in 1837 had been 70 years on the stage, claiming that she had first been carried on in a laundry-basket before she had so much as opened her eyes, but this, possibly, was not strict truth. Born a Lowes, she had fallen in love at first sight, when a teenager, with an actor named Johnston, playing at the time in Wigton. He had courted the girl desperately, but her father had turned him down flat. The girl had then run away from home to join Johnston in Carlisle where he was by that time playing; she arrived wearing all her wardrobe on her person, three dresses and her two best hats, one on top of the other. It had been necessary for her to leave home surreptitiously, without baggage. The runaway had gone to her suitor's lodgings; the horrified landlady there had sent round to the theatre at once for Johnston who had come scurrying immediately, more possibly than not in a state far from overjoyed. We are told that he brought a fellow-actor with him for support; this friend was still in clown's costume and make-up, not having had time to change. The harassed lover and the bewildered clown burst in upon Miss Lowes, seated looking very flushed in her three dresses and two hats. Scarcely had Johnston introduced the clown than Miss Lowes's cousin had arrived, in an enormous flurry, to fetch the young lady home. Johnston began to argue in favour of the cousin and return to the parental roof, but Miss Lowes was adamant; she demanded a Gretna marriage next day and a church ceremony two weeks later after a honeymoon. So great was her force of character that Johnston gave in.

Soon the new Mrs Johnston had found the way on to the boards herself, but she did not stay on them for long. Johnston gave up the stage, or it gave up him; he became a successful auctioneer, using his Shakespeare-voice to great effect in Cumberland salerooms. The Johnstons had ten children; Johnston got himself into debt, he won his case against his creditors, but he had to spend a short time in prison while awaiting hearing of his case and during that time he contracted gaol-fever which killed him soon after his release.

To support her children Mrs Johnston had returned to the stage. She had married another actor, named Deans, who had proved a good business-manager. As Mrs Deans, the lady had played for the next 40 years all over the north, especially in Cumberland and Westmorland, making a point of always avoiding the large towns, possibly because her astute business-manager realised that the company could not stand serious competition in the way of talent, props and so forth.

This, then, was the fabulous Mrs Deans who, when her normal roads were closed, thought nothing of playing Hannibal and leading her company over a mountain-pass. Small wonder that she counted Professor Wilson among her supporters; her *panache* would no doubt have appealed to him enormously. We are a little surprised to hear that Bishop Watson was also a patron of her shows when she played at Ambleside.

It seems astonishing that a tiny place like Mardale should have been worth a visit from Mrs Deans, or Bampton for that matter. The people of Mardale seem, however, to have had a particular zest for life. Like all the dalesfolk of those days they lived hard lives, but they also knew how to enjoy themselves.

The way of life in old Cumberland makes fascinating study. As we have seen, the statesmen supported themselves on small-holdings with which went a flock of sheep. These little farm-houses, at first built of wattle-and-daub or split-laths and daub, were rebuilt, mostly round about mid-seventeenth century, in more solid style; to this period date the typical dale farmsteads with their thick stone walls, recessed slate-seated porches and slate roofs. There was often an outside stair and gallery leading to a long loft where the entire family slept, as in the Icelandic *badstofa*.

My own house is a very good example of such a typical little farm-house. The thick-walled porch had a recessed door, of heavily-studded oak, while at the entry to the porch is still a groove into which could be placed, if necessary, an outer door as extra protection. Within is a large kitchen, at one end of which was a great open fire-place over which was a *rannal-balk* (the beam above which the cheeses were kept). To the left of the fireplace was a small recess in the wall; in this was kept money or valuables. In the ceiling were hooks upon which were suspended home-cured hams and smoked sausages, very long, looped from hook to hook. A friend can remember his old granny hanging these long sausages aloft on hooks in the ceiling; after a certain length of time the sausage became very hard and when the younger members of the family misbehaved the old lady would fetch down a length of sausage and crack the miscreant over the head with it.

On either side of the vast fireplace mutton was hung to smoke; one reads accounts of kitchens where, in winter, as many as seven or eight sheep were hung up thus in the fireplace.

Also above the fireplace was a maiden; a long bar upon which clothes were, and still are, hung to dry.

The floors were first of earth which was freshly strewn with rushes, or sanded, once or twice a week. Later the floors were flag-stoned.

The beams used for building the house are of considerably greater age than the house itself; in all likelihood beams purchased from the Tudor warships when they were broken up. Some of the beams have carving on them; on some are the adze-marks which were used in the old days to hold the plaster. The beams and the surviving original floor-boards are secured not with nails but with wooden pegs. When the old kitchen-ceiling cracked we discovered that the space between the ceiling and the bedroom-floor above was stuffed with ancient oat-husks and cow-dung.

Scratch-tools were used by builders instead of planes; marks of these give indication of the age of the house.

The large kitchen, with niches in the walls for oil-lamps, leads to a stone staircase with a wooden upper flight giving access to a small gallery, stairs and gallery probably having been originally outside the house. Halfway up the stairs a small oak door with a push-up latch reached by shoving one's finger through a hole (in other words the latch is on the inside of the door) gives access to a dark and narrow loft, with a minute window-aperture and a steeply sloping roof which makes it difficult to move about standing upright; this was where the hinds, or farm-hands, slept.

The gallery at the top of the stairs gives access to what was formerly one long large dormitory, the *badstofa*. It would seem that the gallery may also have given access to the adjoining wool-loft.

Below the hinds' loft is a small dairy with a broad slate shelf running round it like a bench; beneath this are the cooling recesses for the dairy-produce, while on the slate bench were laid flitches heaped with brine, brown sugar and spices for curing. The brine got into the walls; they are still holding the damp. Next to the dairy was a smoke-hole. The floor of the dairy and connecting passage are slate-flagged. The partition-wall between the passage and the kitchen is at one point three feet thick.

Adjoining the house at either end was a barn; one of these has now been converted into an extra wing for the house, but the other has roomy byres with a large wool-loft over. A ramp leads to the rear of the barn and rises level with the loft floor so that a cart might convey the wool from the loft with convenience.

The buildings, at the rear, were in fact built into the fell, so that the roof here is only a few feet from the ground while at the front of the house it is some 15 feet or so from the ground; an arrangement that bothered a cat of ours exceedingly when he was an inexperienced kitten. He would leap gaily on to the roof at the back of the house, climb to the top, skip down the other side and find himself, to his horror, peering over a precipice.

The water-supply to the house came from a well in the dairy and from a spring which ran from the fell into a runnel round the back and side of the barn, walled and roofed so that it seems an integral part of the barn.

This, then, was a statesman's home. Lighting was provided by rush-lights and lamps and home-made candles. Peat and wood were burned as fuel. The womenfolk spun and wove, sewed, knitted and quilted. The staple diet was oat-meal porridge, or poddish, enjoyed best 'gey and thick', with butter. Havver-meal was coarse-ground from inferior oats and was the fare of the farm-hands. The maids received a much better quality meal. Havver-cakes were cooked on a smooth flat stone referred to as a backstone. The havver-cake was kept in an oak kist, or cup-board. The meal was kept in a meal-ark; a kind of oak trough on curved legs with a heavy oak lid.

It is interesting that *arval* was the old name for a funeral and that *arval*-bread was funeral bread given to the followers in the open air; one might not eat it on the spot, it had to be carried home and then eaten there.

In accounts of old Cumberland everyone seems to have lived to great ages, remaining amazingly active until the end. Ackermann reported that one medical man attributed this to the thick porridge which the people consumed.

Besides porridge the diet included potatoes, some root vegetables and dried pulses, dairy produce, eggs in the laying-season, smoked pork, bacon, ham and smoked mutton, fresh mutton when it was available. There was very little fruit or green vegetables. Delicacies, apart from tatie-pot, included fat-crowdy, a savoury mess of oatmeal and bone-marrow, which was eaten before meat, cow'd-lword, a pudding of oat-meal, tallow, suet and hog's lard, which sounds pretty awful, and various possets, flavoured with anything sweet from treacle to rum. Also to drink was home-brewed ale. Tea became a great craze in the later half of the nineteenth century when people had discovered that it was something one made a drink out of and not something old women smoked in their cutty-pipes.

There is not room to write here of the many old customs and superstitions which abounded. One can do little but look at the hard days of work; in winter when one rose in the dark to oil-lamps, when twilight descended early in the afternoon upon the little houses tucked under fells and the lamps had to be lit again and life was thus lived all winter-through in what nowadays we, spoilt by electric-light, would consider as semi-darkness. The men worked about the yard and intake-fields, the women in the house. In the evening they spun or weaved, the men made or repaired farm-implements, or fancy walking-sticks. The old aunties made exquisite quilts on quilting-frames, while the old grand-dad told stories, some funny, some sporting, some ghostly. There was much gossiping and chatting and the passing on of news.

In the spring came lambing-time, in the summer the shepherds continued to be busy with the sheep, there was also the hay-making to be done by both sexes and the peat-cutting and drying by the women. In the autumn came the big sheep-gatherings, while the women smoked and cured hams, bacon, mutton in preparation for the winter.

These were the hard days, but there were many merry neets. The Lakeland people were, and still are, very fond of dancing; particularly of three-cornered and eightsome reels in the old days. Fiddlers were much sought-after; not only providing music at the dances and hunt-balls (nothing like so grand as they sound) but also earning themselves reputations as dancing-masters. One such was old Ben Wells, a very well-known and popular dancing-master from Gosforth, renowned for his lively strict-tempo. I have had him described to me as a small, erect, cheerful man who could break up a brawl by playing his fiddle.

The young people, besides dancing, were immensely keen on toffee-joins; get-togethers of lads and lasses in somebody's kitchen, to make toffee and to do a little courting on the side. One still meets old ladies who, suddenly animated, will start telling stories of long-distant toffee-joins.

These were indoor sports. Outdoor sports included wrestling, cock-fighting, ratting, hound-trails, skating in the winter, and of course hunting, fishing and racing. The most popular events of the year were the shepherds' meets; the large meets took place (still do take place) in the autumn. Those held in the summer-months were simply for the exchange of stray sheep; one such is held on Walna Scar. But the big, convivial meets were held in the back-end: I must repeat that these meets flourish today as strongly as ever they did.

There were certain classical places for these meets; the great one of the year in the distant past was held on High Street, whence barrels of beer, huge pies and tatie-pots were conveyed, and sports were held, including horse-racing (the top of High Street is surprisingly level). Then the breed of shepherds weakened, the Meet repaired to the Old Dun Bull at Mardale. This remained the great place for the annual meet for over a hundred years, until the drowning of Mardale. The Kirkstone Inn was another great place for meets and so is the Woolpack at Eskdale.

The official business of the meet is the collecting of all the stray sheep that have been found on the fells and the return of them to their owners. But there is more to a meet than simple business. There is always a fox-hunt; in the Dun Bull days, when the meet lasted two days, Joe Bowman, the famous huntsman of the Ullswater, used to lead the two days' hunting, singing and celebrating all night, but out hunting by eight in the morning. There is also wrestling, the famous game of face-pulling, there used to be cock-fighting. However, there is no gainsaying that the merry neet which follows the sporting day is *the* feature of a shepherds' meet. Ladies are not admitted to merry neets (if they were then the neets would doubtless lose much of their merriment, which would be a great pity), so one has only garbled accounts of what goes on. Certainly great quantities of food and drink are consumed, and there are innumerable toasts and stories and choruses, including one to Joe Bowman, as well as other hunting-choruses of, I believe, often brilliantly improvised nature. But as I say, these are masculine occasions; one only really knows details of the menu, which always includes tatie-pots, apple-pie and cheese and plenty of ale to drink. The dinner is presided over by a chairman.

The truth is, of course, that the holiday-visitor learns very little of the real life of the dales. There are now two Lakelands; the tourist Lakeland and the Lakeland which comes to life after the visitors have all gone home at the summer's end. During the bracken-months this Lakeland lies submerged, as old Mardale lies submerged, but just as the spirit which imbued Mardale has survived in the District, although Mardale itself has been lost, so does this summertime-submerged Lakeland come back to life each year as soon as the traffic has cleared and the postcard-racks have been taken from the shop-fronts and carried inside. Now the little towns belong to the townspeople again. Sales and coffee-mornings start to be advertised, there are dances and whist-drives, societies hold meetings. The campers and caravanners vanish, the hairy-legged hikers are gone, instead fox-hunters are out and about. Everything settles into quite a different tempo. The bracken turns gold and bronze and dries to brittle rusty stems, spiders weave October webs, silver with dew, the first frosts come. Although it is colder the skies become higher and clearer. The best time of the year has arrived, the back-end, time of shepherds' meets and merry neets.

CHAPTER ELEVEN

The Caldbeck Fells and Penrith —A Way Out

Your trip to the Lake District is also nearly at an end, another day or so, and you will be gone in your turn. I regret it, for there are a lot of places you have not yet seen, a lot of things you have not done. You have not climbed Black Combe, for example, that magic mountain of Skiddaw slate that has somehow escaped from the rest of that ancient rock and has appeared between the Duddon estuary and the Irish Sea. Upon its flank is the Swinside stone-circle, nearly 100 yards in circumference and locally known as the Sunkenkirk. The black combe which gives the mountain its name lies on the south-east side of the fell, near the top. At Black Combe the bees sing at 12 midnight on Christmas Eve and the cattle kneel in adoration. Also, 'in what quarter soever a bull lies facing, Allhallowe'en thence will blow the prevailing wind', say the sages of Black Combe. Hob Thrust, or Hob Thross, 'a body all over rough', is the Black Combe familiar; in the old days in the small hours he would do your work for you if you left him out a platter of thick porridge with plenty of butter in it.

The dead in this part of the world were always waked. Money could only be lent at Candlemas, servants were hired only at Martinmas and Whitsuntide. On Christmas morning the local dish was hack-pudding, made of sheep's heart, suet and dried fruit, a very ancient dish that might have been rather good.

Newlyweds never bought corn for their first sowing; they went corn-laiting (meaning searching or seeking for corn), travelling around the locality with a sack which they filled with corn begged off their neighbours. Had they purchased the corn they would have grown no crop, nor would they ever prosper in life.

I ask you where *you* would like to go for your last day in the District and you reply, rather to my surprise and, perhaps, annoyance, that you would like to go to Troutbeck to see where John Peel came from. Well, then let us go, but I must warn you first of all that he came from Caldbeck, not Troutbeck; Caldbeck that lies 'back o' Skidda'. He was born there and buried there, you will see his grave, and he spent his life hunting foxes and begetting children, 13 of them. He was a statesman, certainly not in any great financial position and quite how he managed to keep his farm going, support his large family and hunt all day every day for the greater part of the year is somewhat of a mystery: he had a pack of his own, of some sort or other, for over 50 years. He hunted the low-country on horseback and the high fells on foot, wearing corduroy knee-breeches, stockings, a long grey coat and a tall, light-coloured beaver hat. He had very long legs and a prodigious thirst. He would start hunting at daybreak, be out all day, walking upwards perhaps of 40 miles, spend the night drinking and singing with his cronies while his wet hunting clothes dried on him; he would then fall asleep with his clothes on, lie like a log through the small hours, then be up at dawn to go hunting again. Pneumonia, I am told, was the occupational-disease of these old huntsmen; Peel seems never to have succumbed.

Lakeland hunting-people doubt that Peel was really so great a huntsman as Joe Bowman of the Ullswater, John Crozier of the Blencathra, or Tommy Dobson or Willie Porter of Eskdale. Peel is in fact dismissed in some local circles, by people whose grand-parents can recall first-hand accounts of him, with the phrase, 'Nobbut a drunken old teggelt'.

Then how did he become so famous? The answer perhaps is simple; Peel had a first-rate P.R.O.

This was his friend, John Woodcock Graves, with whom Peel used to drink at the local inn of an evening, bragging of the numbers of foxes he had caught. I have no doubt that Graves got fed up with this and said, drily, 'Aye, ye're a great man, John' and went on to say that he ought to have a song about him. He then began to fiddle about with a refrain, 'D'ye ken John Peel?' singing the words to himself, to the music of an old lullaby, *Bonnie Annie*, which an old woman, it is said, was at that moment crooning to a sleeping baby in another part of the room. Peel meantime was chuckling and exclaiming, mightily satisfied to be having a song made about him. And so, as a joke rather than anything else, the song was drafted out by the two friends, and presently Peel staggered home singing it.

But it was not, at first, a very successful song; a hunting-song written to a lullaby sounds not quite right, even at this distance in time. It was not until 1868 that William Metcalfe, the choirmaster at Carlisle cathedral, re-arranged the setting and the song at last soared to success. By that time Peel was dead, but the song brought him world-wide posthumous fame which he certainly would not have had otherwise and very possibly did not deserve in the slightest. It is that 'Tally-ho!' which makes the song so irresistible both to men at merry neets and Scouts round camp-fires.

You could do worse than spend your last day in the District exploring the country back o' Skidda; lonely, perfectly unspoilt. From there you could drive to Penrith, an historic Border town which was many times raided by the Scots. The country here boasts of several surviving pele-towers. You must be feeling that you have travelled in somewhat of a circle; invading Scots and pele-towers are where you came in, you say. Not quite, for you are in Cumberland, but if you drive across Shap fells you will soon be in Kendal.

From Kendal you will take the road south, still singing 'D'ye ken John Peel' to yourself with the distaste one feels for a maddening tune one cannot get out of one's mind. But, as the days pass following your return from the Lake District, you will find that there are many things which, maddeningly, you can't forget; the lonely bleating of sheep up a beck, the smell of northern upland turf, the long shafts of reflected light on Ullswater, the warm sandstone walls of Furness Abbey. These memories will come back repeatedly, so that it is perfectly understandable if you find yourself, far sooner than you had ever intended, driving northwards again, perhaps in a different season of the year this time, and you have bought yourself a pair of boots. At these I look with approval. Boots. You are going to walk. At last you will really see the Lake District.

Index

The numerals in **heavy type** refer to the *figure numbers* of the illustrations

213

Index

Stybarrow Crag, 188
Sty Head, 138, 145, 185; Tarn, 44, 141, 185
Summit cairns, 44
Sunday Crag, St, 80, 188
Surrey, Earl of, 32, 188
Sussex, Earl of, 47
Sutton, Graham, 155
Swaledale Sheep, 19
Swindale, 201
Swinside stone circle, 26
Swirrel Edge, 196
Symonds, H. H. (qu.), *Walking in the Lake District*, 19, 21, 155

Taillebois, Ivo and Emily de, 32
Taylor, Dr Michael W., 193
Taylor Ghyll Force, 44
Thirlmere, 161, 164, 180, 189, 191, 196
Thomas, Mr E., 158
Thornythwaite, 142; Hall, 201
Three Shire Stone, 99, 107
Threlkeld, 124
Throstle Garth, 108, 114
Thurland, Thomas, 172
Till, William, 171
'Toffee-joins' (social gatherings), 207
Tolson, Hall, 36
Tolson, Thomas, 36
Tongue Beck, 154
Tophet Wall, 147
Torver, 53
Townend, Troutbeck, 75
Town End, Kendal, 33
Traverse, the (Gable), 146, 154
Trimmer, Samuel (quarryman), 157
Troutbeck, 40, 73, 192, 211; Tongue, 189
Tulketh, 42
Tups, 122
Turner, J. M. W., 63
Twinters, 122
Tyndall, Professor, 133
Tynwald Hill, Isle of Man, 107
Tyson, Dame Anne, 81, 82; family, 134; Towers, 126

Ullscarf, 99
Ullswater, 22, 26, Chap. X
Ulpha Fell, 99, 108
Ulverston, 53

Vallon, Annette, 84, 89, 91; Caroline (Wordsworth's illegitimate daughter), 85
Verdon, 180
Vikings, 22, 27, 42, 60, 107, 116, 118, 180

Wadd (plumbago) smuggling, 155, 183, 184
Wade, General, 33
'Wade's Road', 33
Wake, funeral, 210
Wakefield, Dr, 158
Walker's Gully, 158
Wall End, 103
Walls, stone, 113
Walnar Scar, 53, 207; pony track, 54
Walton, J., 65; William de, 69
Wandope, 185
Wansfell, 73; Pike, 73
Ward, Mrs Humphrey, *Helbeck of Bannisdale*, 31
Warnscale Bottom, 186
Wasdale, 23, 44, Chap. VII; Head, 44, 115, 118, 128, 137, 146, 147, 154, 155, 160
Wastwater, 116, 117, 138; 17; Screes, 117
Wastwater Hotel, 134
Watendlath, 69, 180, 183
Waterhead, 66, 72
Wells, Ben (fiddler), 207
Westmorland, 22, 23; Crags, 146
Westmorland Gazette, 36
West Wall (Scafell), 144; Traverse, 158
Wetherlam, 59, 99
Whillan Beck, 113
Whinfell Hall, 147
Whinlatter Fells, 22; Pass, 161, 185
Whisky-distilling, illicit, 104, 155
Whitehaven, 57, 107; coalfield, 24; Iron Mine Company, 110

223

(overleaf) *The Langdale Pikes*